EVERYTHING YOU NEED TO KNOW

CAR COLLECTING

STEVE LINDEN

MOTORBOOKS

First published in 2008 by Motorbooks, an imprint of MBI Publishing Company LLC, Galtier Plaza, Suite 200, 380 Jackson Street, St. Paul, MN 55101 USA

Motorbooks titles are also available at discounts in bulk quantity for industrial or sales-promotional use. For details write to Special Sales Manager at MBI Publishing Company, Galtier Plaza, Suite 200, 380 Jackson Street, St. Paul, MN 55101 USA.

To find out more about our books, join us online at www.motorbooks.com.

About the author: Steve Linden grew up in a time and place where cars were worshipped, and none more so than the American car. His father enjoyed nice, fast cars, and he and Steve spent many evenings and weekends in the family garage tending to them. By the age of twelve, Steve was repairing just about anything with an engine.

Recognizing Steve's early need for speed, his father strongly "suggested" a 1967 Lincoln Continental as Steve's first car, believing that his son would be best protected in a "tank." But high performance prevailed, and the Lincoln was followed shortly by a 1970 Mustang, a 1964 LeMans, and a memorable yellow 1970 Cuda. Over one hundred cars have since followed.

In addition to writing and cars, Steve is an avid classic motorcycle collector. He provides expert witness testimony in court cases involving collector cars, and he is a classic automobile appraiser. He currently lives on Long Island with his wife, Pam, son Josh, dog Sky, and a small stable of fine automobiles and motorcycles.

On the cover: First generation Corvettes are a favorite at every car show.

On the frontispiece: The Shelby Cobra is one of the most collectible American cars of all time.

On the title pages:
(left) Perhaps your first car was the old family station wagon your parents gave you because they felt it was safe. But you really wanted something the girls would like—a new 1963 Corvette split-window coupe. Unfortunately, you didn't get it then, but now, you can.

(middle left) Z is for Zagato. Zagato began his career in 1919 as a coachbuilder. Coachbuilders would begin with a chassis that was supplied by a manufacturer and add the body, interior, and sometimes the powertrain. Zagato's specialty was performance, particularly aerodynamics.

(middle right) A basic restoration to high-quality driver standards would include things such as having the car painted, having the interior reupholstered, replacing the chrome, and doing all the mechanical work necessary to make the car 100 percent functional. This restoration may cost $25,000 or more depending on the condition and complexity of the car, as well as availability of parts.

(right) Buy low, sell high! Easier said than done. The buying part is easy. It's the selling part that's hard. Collector cars may be undervalued for any number of reasons. Season, location, or the seller's need to dispose of the car quickly may affect prices. You could buy Porsche Speedster convertibles during a Northeast winter and sell them in Southern California where they are more highly valued.

On the back cover:
(top left) Shelbys are highly collectible and in great demand—and their prices reflect it!

(top right) Muscle cars equipped with big-block engines are extremely desirable.

(bottom left) Don't be fooled by an immaculate interior or flashy paint. Always perform a pre-purchase inspection.

(bottom right) The value of a collector car is often impacted by geography and sometimes even by season.

Library of Congress Cataloging-in-Publication Data

Linden, Steve, 1957-
  Car collecting: everything you need to know / by Steve Linden.
    p. cm.
  ISBN-13: 978-0-7603-2809-5 (softbound)
  ISBN-10: 0-7603-2809-9 (softbound)
  1. Antique and classic cars—Collectors and collecting—Amateurs' manuals.
  I. Title.
  TL7.A1L56 2008
  629.222075—dc22
                          2007046683

Editor: Chris Endres
Designer: Brenda C. Canales

Printed in Singapore

CONTENTS

Introduction

Pride of ownership and pleasure of use. These are the answers that I always receive when I ask newcomers and veterans what they enjoy most about the collector car hobby. Collector cars are every bit as diverse as the people who participate in the hobby, meaning there is truly a collector car for everyone. Whether you're a Baby Boomer who wants to relive fond automotive memories with your children or a die-hard muscle car fanatic who wants to spend every waking moment in your garage, there's a collector car out there for you.

One thing that makes collector cars so appealing is that they stand out from the crowd. Try placing a 1965 Mustang in a parking lot with one thousand modern cars. Your three-year-old child and your half-blind, 85-year-old grandmother will readily pick out the Mustang. They may not know exactly what it is, but they'll know it's different.

The universal appeal of a collector car will embolden absolute strangers to walk right up to you and begin a conversation because they know they will be warmly received. Passing motorists will often give you the thumbs-up, and children will yell "Nice car!" at traffic lights. For many years, my wife drove a bright yellow Volkswagen Karmann Ghia convertible. I can't remember one outing when a child didn't happily say her car looked like half a lemon.

One of the wonderful things about this hobby is that you can choose the level of participation right for you. You can buy a modestly priced driver-quality car that you can hop in at will and drive to the mall, or you can buy a trailer queen that will require you to place carpet on the ground, lest the tires come in contact with pavement.

Pride, pleasure, diversity, camaraderie, uniqueness are just some of the no-cost options that come with collector car ownership. Everybody has individual reasons for wanting a collector car, and no single reason is more valid than any other. Ultimately, it's all about how it makes you feel.

Owning a collector car, and the endless enjoyment that goes along with that ownership, is separate and distinct from the process of buying it. Buying a collector car can be anything but endless enjoyment if the correct decisions are not made before and during the purchasing stage. However, making the correct decisions is not as difficult as you might think. If you succeed in making

the correct decisions—and you will—your collector car should bring you many years and many miles of pleasure and pride of ownership.

This book will help you to identify decisions you will have to make and give you information you will need to make those decisions correctly. You will be able to avoid the pitfalls that await you, whether you are a first-time buyer or a seasoned collector. After all, there is no reason buying a collector car should not be as enjoyable as owning a collector car. Hopefully, this book will add to that enjoyment.

Chapter 1

WHAT IS A COLLECTOR CAR AND WHICH ONE IS RIGHT FOR YOU?

WHAT YOU WILL LEARN:

- The definition of a collector car

- How to make your purchase a positive experience

- How to choose the right car for you

The 1957 Chevrolet Bel Air is one of the most recognizable and desirable collector cars of all time. It has stood the test of time and transcended generations of collectors. It is prized today by young and old collectors alike. You will see examples of these cars that have undergone painstaking restorations to original condition, as well as others that have been restored as the hot rods that made them so popular in the 1950s.

Collector cars come in all shapes and sizes, such as this 1967 Mustang. Mustangs are part of a group of cars called "pony cars"—a term that originated with the Mustang.

COLLECTOR CAR DEFINED

A collector car is almost anything you want it to be. It can be an antique car, such as a 1931 LaSalle. It can be a muscle car, such as a 1970 Chevelle SS. It can be a pony car, such as a 1967 Mustang GT Fastback. It can be a modern classic car, such as a 2003 Plymouth Prowler. It can be a 1953 Allard race car.

However, a car doesn't have to be old, rare, new, or fast to be a collector car. It could also be a 1970 Dodge Dart or a 1971 Oldsmobile Vista Cruiser Station Wagon with the funny raised roof and window just behind the front seats. It might also be a 1923 Ford T-Bucket—the kind you see at many car shows. It could be the 1953 Chevy Pickup Truck

Is the Amphicar a car used as a boat or a boat driven like a car? Either way, these unusual cars are sure to attract attention as you drive right down the launch ramp and into the water. Although they perform adequately on land and water, they do not excel at either. Don't plan on pulling any water skiers with your Amphicar.

that's been sitting in your barn since 1970. It could be a 1964 Impala SS or a 1994 Impala SS. It could be a 1970 Ferrari Daytona or a 1990 Dodge Daytona. In fact, it doesn't even have to be all car! It could be a half-car, half-boat 1964 Amphicar. It need not have four wheels. It can be a three-wheeled 1937 Morgan. It can run on gasoline, alcohol, gasohol, diesel, methanol, steam, kerosene, electricity, or sunlight.

MAKE YOUR PURCHASE A POSITIVE EXPERIENCE

For most people, buying a collector car represents a major investment of money and time, much like buying a home. To ensure a positive outcome, you will need to begin to understand a bit about yourself, your likes, and your dislikes. There are many, many different types of collector cars, and deciding what is right for you is of paramount importance.

What makes a car collectible?

Answer: People collect them. That is not to say every car you may purchase is a collector car. The operative word is "collect." Someone will collect virtually every car from every manufacturer—from Abarth to Zil. Visit a car show or a cruise night, and you will see this yourself. Although more people collect Ford Mustangs than AMC Pacers, this does not make a Mustang more collectible than a Pacer, if you happen to like Pacers. It certainly does have other implications, such as price and availability.

Muscle cars are large, powerful cars that carry at least four people comfortably. Built between the early 1960s and the early 1970s, they are generally equipped with a big-block engine and often come with a four-speed transmission. This 1969 Plymouth Sport Satellite is an example of an American muscle car.

Who says a car needs to have four wheels? This is a 1934 Morgan SS. Morgans are very collectible, even though it is sometimes difficult to tell which way they're going. By the way, the single wheel is at the rear of the car.

Perhaps fins, chrome, and leather are more your style. The 1959 Cadillac El Dorado defines the word opulence. But be forewarned, this car is so large that it will not fit in many standard-size garages.

Over the years, I have come to understand there are three critical questions you must answer to ensure you will realize a positive outcome.

What do you like?
What are you going to use it for?
How much do you want to spend?

A clear understanding of these three questions and their answers forms the foundation for a positive experience in the purchase of a collector vehicle. When you first decide you want to buy a collector car, you may be unable to answer one or more of these three questions. That's OK. We'll explore these three questions in a little more detail.

WHAT DO YOU LIKE?

You would be surprised at how many people can't answer this question. This is the most important question you must answer before you start the search for a collector car. If

Not all collector cars are American. This 1955 Citroën Traction Avant was technologically advanced for its time. It had a modern four-cylinder engine and front-wheel drive.

You never know what you'll find when you are searching for a collector car. This car was spotted at a local car show, and even the owner, who was also the builder, wasn't sure exactly what it was. It's not likely you'll ever see another one, so this must be a very collectible car!

There are collector cars from A to Z. A is for Abarth. In the 1960s, Abarth was quite successful in hill-climbing and sports-car racing, mainly in classes up to 2,000cc. The company competed with Porsche and Ferrari.

you are not sure how to answer this question, maybe I can help.

As applied to collector cars, most people like something that elicits a certain emotion. This emotion is different for everybody. To answer this question, let's start with another question. What

prompted you to want a collector car in the first place? Here are some of the more popular answers I hear.

"I had one of those when I was 17, and I always wanted another one." (Good answer.)

Z is for Zagato. Zagato began his career in 1919 as a coachbuilder. Coachbuilders would begin with a chassis that was supplied by a manufacturer and add the body, interior, and sometimes the powertrain. Zagato's specialty was performance, particularly aerodynamics.

Collector cars can represent a major investment—sometimes more than a house. This is a Hispano Suiza which can easily reach into the hundreds of thousands of dollars and sometimes exceed $1,000,000. Whether you are spending $10,000 or $1,000,000, it is important to determine what you like before spending any money at all.

"I didn't have one of those when I was 17, and I always wanted one." (Good answer.)

"My dad had one of those when I was a kid, and it brings back memories." (Good answer.)

"I don't know why I want a collector car, they just look like fun." (O.K. answer.)

"My neighbors—the Joneses—just bought a collector car, so I need one." (Bad answer.)

"I want to be able to take the family out to a cruise night on a nice summer evening." (Good answer.)

"I think it would be a good investment." (Bad answer, at least if you're reading this book. Leave the investing to the dealers. More about that later.)

"Girls like guys with shiny, old convertibles." (Good answer. I mean bad answer.)

Deciding what is right for you is paramount for a satisfying result. Although you may have always dreamed of owning a Bugatti, this may not be a wise decision if your family is included in your weekend plans.

"I've always enjoyed working on cars. I have a couple of extra bucks and some extra time."
(OK answer. As long as you're aware of what you are getting into.)

Some of these answers may apply to you, or they may not. You will have to determine what vehicle you like before you start your search. That is not to say you have to decide the year, make, and model. You do not have to be able to say, "I want a 1929 Duesenberg Model J LeBaron dual-cowl Phaeton," although, it would be nice if you could.

It would be helpful, however, if you could say, "I like old pickup trucks," or "I like red convertibles." The more specific, the better. For example, do you like red Corvette

Before you start your search, determine what type of car you like. It is not necessary to be able to identify a specific year, make, and model, such as a 1929 Duesenberg Model J LeBaron dual-cowl phaeton, but it would be nice if you could.

Some people were lucky enough to have owned a classic muscle car, such as this 1967 Pontiac GTO, at some point in their youth. The desire to re-live that thrill has made early GTOs some of the most sought-after collector cars ever.

convertibles or red Lincoln Continental convertibles? The differences are very important!

Let me illustrate. The Corvette is small; the Lincoln is large. The Corvette has two doors; the Lincoln has four doors. The Corvette seats two; the Lincoln seats six. The Corvette has no trunk; the Lincoln has a trunk large enough to hold the Corvette.

For obvious reasons, the more specific you can be, the better. You might be slightly disappointed if you really want a little red Corvette convertible and purchase a big red Lincoln Continental convertible by accident. How do you make sure this doesn't happen? You educate yourself. This is the fun part because, in reality, most people have a pretty good idea of what they like but just don't know it.

In this case, education might consist of looking at a large number of books and magazines. However, you probably do not want to do this quite yet. If you do look through

Perhaps your first car was the old family station wagon your parents gave you because they felt it was safe. But you really wanted something the girls would like—a new 1963 Corvette split-window coupe. Unfortunately, you didn't get it then, but now you can.

Perhaps nostalgia is the reason you want a collector car. That same station wagon you were embarrassed to drive to high school now brings back fond memories of family road trips. Classic station wagons are becoming more popular every year. They are reminiscent of an era gone by, yet at the same time, they are functional and family-friendly.

"Keeping up with the Joneses." This is not the best motive for buying a collector car, but if it's the only one you have, you're probably the type of person who will outdo your neighbor. Few cars can make a statement like a Cobra—real or replica. Just park it in a prominent position in your driveway. You don't even have to drive it.

books, you will probably find yourself drawn to a huge number of cars. Buying a collector car is an emotional event or, at least, should be. Simply viewing cars in a book removes the emotional component from the purchasing experience.

The best way to find out what stimulates these emotions is to look at the cars themselves. Go to a car show or a cruise night. Do not go to shows sponsored by marque-specific car clubs, such as the Corvette Club of America, the Mustang Club of America, or the Auburn-Cord-Duesenberg Club. This may come later, but for now, it is best to be exposed to a broad range of cars.

On any given weekend, there are probably many car shows you are not even aware of within an hour's drive of your home. Go to a few of these shows. Walk around, look at the cars, and talk

Your tastes may lean toward a small, two-seat sports car like this early Corvette. Just make sure you won't need to carry more than one passenger or a set of golf clubs, or your low-mileage Corvette will remain a low-mileage Corvette when your family wants to come along.

Cruise Nights can also be held during the day. They are a great way to get family and friends together. Many towns will close the main street to traffic, allowing pedestrians to wander among the cars. There is no judging and no trophies—just a relaxed environment where the cars are the stars. Pop into the local soda shop for a root beer float and enjoy the warm summer evening.

to the owners. The owners love to talk, and talk, and talk. In fact, usually they won't stop talking. However, this is a good thing. More on this later.

You'll have an opportunity to see many different kinds of cars at a show or cruise night. I guarantee that, after attending a few of these events, you will have a much better, clearer, and more specific idea of which cars elicit those all-important emotions. I cannot overstress the importance of this. Ultimately, when you finally do purchase a collector car, you will want to experience those emotions every time you drive it. And, if you make all the right decisions, you will!

HOW WILL YOU USE IT?

The second question to answer is "What are you going to use it for?" Once again, I can't answer this question for you, but I can help by giving you some possible answers. You know best what you are going to use it for, and that is what counts. As you read some of these possible answers, it should become obvious why this question is so important. If it doesn't, don't worry, I'll tell you later.

"I'm going to pile the family into it, including the St. Bernard, and go to the beach."
(Good answer. Seriously. I believe that cars were meant to be used—as long as you buy the right car.)

"I want to take it to cruise nights and local car shows."
(Good answer.)

"I want to enter it in competition on a national level."
(Good answer. You may not know what you're in for, but your heart's in the right place.)

Some people enjoy the roominess only a large car provides. A large Lincoln will likely be equipped with luxury options a Corvette will not have. Large cars are particularly useful if you have a large family and need ample room in the trunk for weekend getaways. This car will seat six people comfortably.

"I want a car that I can spend some time restoring."
(Good answer, depending on how you define "some time." This often ends up being defined as a "lifetime.")

"I want to put my company's logo on the side and use it for business."
(Good answer and becoming much more popular. Did I just give you an idea?)

"I just want something that I can enjoy on weekends."
(Good answer.)

"I want to use it as a daily driver. I think that I can buy a collector car for less than the price of a new car."
(Good answer and also becoming more popular.)

Attend shows that have broader arrays of collector cars. You'll have opportunities to see cars from many manufacturers in different models and body styles.

Do not go to a marque-specific car show at this early stage in your search for a collector car. This will limit your exposure to the vast array of available cars. Once you've narrowed your search, these shows can be valuable tools.

"I want to buy it as an investment." (Bad answer. This is your second warning. We'll talk about this later.)

Like everything else in life, if you make a significant investment in an item, you will want to use that item for its intended purpose. That's why I asked you "What are you going to use it for?"

For example, let's say you enjoy boats. You get a great deal on a 46-foot Chris-Craft offshore fishing boat. It's in great shape, has everything from twin engines to GPS, and can carry 10 of your friends 70 miles offshore for a weekend fishing trip. The only problem is that you live in the middle of Iowa. Suddenly, it's not such a great deal.

The same concept applies to collector cars. If you have a family of six, not including the dog, and you want to use your collector car to take day trips on weekends, you'd best put that little red Corvette convertible on the back burner and think about that big red Lincoln convertible. The little red Corvette will look great in your garage, and that is where it will remain. You'll start to resent the Corvette every weekend you pull away from home in your minivan for that day trip. You'll also start to resent your family for not fitting into the Corvette. Last, but

If you enjoy packing a picnic and heading to the beach with the family and the dog, a woody may be just the vehicle for you. Don't forget to strap the surfboard to the roof.

not least, you'll start to resent yourself for not buying the Lincoln.

But don't be disheartened. You can always buy the Corvette as your second collectible car, and trust me, you will eventually own a second collectible car. People who get into this hobby invariably get "the sickness." You will, too. Unfortunately, there is no known cure.

Talk with the owners of the cars that appeal to you. Try to find out the positive aspects as well as the negative aspects of owning that particular vehicle. Owners of these cars love to talk, and talk, and talk. They will offer a wealth of information.

You may want to buy a collector car because you'll enjoy the fun and camaraderie of entering a judged show. Beware: competition can be fierce even at a local level, where the caliber of cars can be very high.

Competition at a national level can be incredibly expensive and time-consuming. Cars receive points for competition in certain shows, and to be competitive, you must be prepared to have your car transported around the country. Rarely is the financial reward equal to the outlay. It is done for the love of the hobby and competitive spirit.

Old pickup trucks are becoming very popular as collector vehicles. While most will only seat three people, they are very useful and can earn their keep. They are also a relative bargain in the collector car market.

Many owners are choosing to use their collector cars as daily drivers. If properly maintained, these cars are remarkably dependable. They also offer many of the creature comforts of modern cars, such as air conditioning. Before these cars were collectible, they were daily drivers.

Woulda, Coulda, Shoulda

Mark had been told all his life he was the type of person who marched to the beat of his own drummer. This may very well have been true because Mark had always liked Volkswagen Karmann Ghia convertibles. They are kind of offbeat, you rarely see them nowadays, and when you do, it draws everybody's attention. Mark not only liked the way they looked, he also liked the unmistakable sound that only a Volkswagen air-cooled engine makes. Additionally, they are relatively inexpensive and use very little gas.

Mark was hoping to be lucky enough to find a nice one that he would actually be able to use on his weekend errands. Mark told some of his friends he was considering buying a collector car. He didn't mention he liked Karmann Ghias for fear they might laugh at him.

Somehow, all of Mark's friends convinced him he needed a 1970 Chevelle SS with a 454 engine and a four-speed transmission—preferably in black. Unfortunately for Mark, they found one for him. Even more unfortunately, he bought it.

He wasn't that proficient at driving a high performance four-speed, and truth be told, he was a little intimidated by the car. It was too fast, too loud, and too expensive for him to enjoy. In the two years Mark owned the car, he drove it exactly four times. Two of those times were for the mandatory yearly state inspections.

Mark finally sold the car and, shortly thereafter, bought a Karmann Ghia convertible. To this day, you can see Mark driving his Karmann Ghia around town every chance he gets, with his sunglasses on and a smile on his face.

Buying a collector car as an investment is best left to professionals. However, if the investment component of ownership is important to you, rarity and provenance are two things to take into consideration. This Chrysler concept car has plenty of both.

People who get into this hobby for the right reasons in the right manner will often end up owning a second collector car. This is known as "the sickness." Unfortunately, there is no known cure, so you had best make sure you have room for more than one.

HOW MUCH TO SPEND?

You want to spend as much as you can for any given car. Buy the best car that you can afford.

It does not make financial sense to buy a collector car that needs significant repairs or restoration. There are those who would disagree with me on this point. But trust me, I'm right. They're wrong. This is a very important point, so let me clarify it somewhat. I'm right! They're wrong! OK, now that it's clear, I will admit there are always exceptions, but they are few and far between.

For the most part, these exceptions only apply to mechanics (with a lot of spare time on their hands), body men (with a lot of spare time on their hands), and people who have inherited a bunch of junky old cars, all of the same make and model (with a lot of spare time on their hands). In some rare instances, it may make sense to do repairs or a restoration on a collector car, and we'll discuss these cases later.

Just in case I haven't convinced you, ponder this. If you inherited a

Unless you are highly skilled and have a lot of spare time, it does not make financial sense to restore a car in this condition. If you have to buy the parts and pay somebody to do the labor, the cost of the restoration will exceed the value of the car. Believe it or not, this 1969 Camaro recently sold for $6,900.

This 1969 Camaro is the same year, make, and model as in the previous picture. A restoration to these standards can easily exceed $50,000, yet cars in this condition can be purchased for as little as $25,000. It is wise to buy the best car you can afford.

1969 Mustang Mach 1—as in, got it for free—that was in need of a complete restoration, you would be better off selling it for parts. You could purchase a completely restored car of the same year, make, and model for less than it would cost you to restore your free car! So, buy the best car you can afford. In most cases, you will find you have to do some repairs or minor restoration anyway. From a financial perspective, it pays to keep these to a minimum. We'll get into the topic of repairing and restoring a collector car versus buying a restored one a little later on.

You will have to decide whether to buy a convertible or a hardtop. Driving a convertible on a warm, sunny day is guaranteed to provide you with plenty of warmth and sunshine. But if you are the type of person who would rather drive in air-conditioned comfort, a convertible may not be for you.

When the top goes down, the price goes up. A car like this Jaguar XK-E roadster is valued at upwards of $50,000. If it were a coupe, it would be worth approximately half that.

CONVERTIBLE OR HARDTOP?

One decision you will ultimately make is whether you want to buy a convertible or a sedan. When people envision themselves driving their dream cars, it is often with the wind blowing through their hair on a warm, sunny day. There is absolutely no denying the experience of driving a convertible is reason enough to buy one. However, there are other factors to consider.

Generally speaking, given the same year, make, and model of collector car, the convertible will be more expensive. The premium you will pay for a convertible will generally be in the range of 10 to 30 percent. Depending on the rarity of the car, the premium may reach 200%, or even more. For example, a documented Pontiac GTO Judge may be worth $75,000, whereas, a documented Pontiac GTO Judge convertible may be worth $300,000 or more. As a rule, when the top goes down, the price goes up!

A convertible lacks one of the most important structural components of any car—a roof. Because it lacks a roof, a convertible tends to flex when going over rough surfaces. Most manufacturers tried to minimize this problem by adding structural reinforcements elsewhere in the car, usually underneath the floors, but this flexing will often manifest itself in all sorts of noises, such as squeaks and rattles. These noises are generally less noticeable when the top is down.

These numbers are stamped on the block of a Chevrolet Corvette. The last six digits of the smaller number on the right must match the last six digits of the vehicle identification number. If they don't, the car is not numbers-matching. The numbers and letters on the left contain additional information used for verification.

This same lack of structural rigidity also tends to have a negative impact on the vehicle's handling characteristics. Because the suspension's geometry is often changing in response to a flexing chassis, the handling will generally not be as precise as it would be for the same model of vehicle in hardtop form. In reality, this is not a consideration for most drivers because they will not be driving their collector cars aggressively.

Styling is another major consideration. Convertible tops are designed to be functional and generally detract from the aesthetics of the collector car, at least in the raised position.

If you are the type of person who would rather drive in air-conditioned comfort, a convertible may not be the car for you. In reality, driving your convertible on a warm, sunny day is guaranteed to provide you with plenty of two things—warmth and sun. Air conditioning is not a very common option in convertibles old enough to be considered collectible. Prior to the 1950s, air conditioning was virtually nonexistent. In the 1960s and 1970s, air conditioning became more popular, but it was still rarely ordered on convertibles. Naturally there are exceptions, but convertibles of this era often carry a significant premium in price if they are equipped with air conditioning, even if it doesn't work.

Convertibles must be inspected very carefully prior to purchase. Almost all convertibles considered collector cars leak water to some degree and, therefore, are very prone to rust in certain areas.

OPTIONAL EQUIPMENT

In general, the more options a collector car has, the more desirable it

A well-optioned car will generally be worth more than the same make and model with fewer options. This is the interior of a well-optioned 1972 Mercury Cougar convertible with air conditioning, AM-FM stereo radio, console, power windows, remote mirror, and power seats.

is. Given two collector cars differing only in options, the higher-optioned car will sell for more money.

There are some collector cars one would expect to have certain options, and lack of these options might actually detract from the value of a car or make it more difficult to sell. For example, although Cadillac was always the flagship of General Motors, items like air conditioning were not always standard equipment. Nowadays, classic Cadillacs not equipped with air conditioning will typically be more difficult to sell and will usually sell at a discount.

Exceptions to this rule are what are known as delete options. On some cars, typically muscle cars or those that might be used for high-performance purposes, the option of deleting some standard equipment, such as radios or heaters, was actually offered to the purchaser. You could actually instruct the factory not to install these items. Naturally, most people would not choose to remove something that was standard. If one can document that the items missing from the car were actually delete options at the factory level, and not simply

Can you spot the difference between these two cars? Most people can't. One of these cars has matching numbers and one doesn't. What does this mean? It means the numbers-matching car is worth about $65,000—about twice that of the other.

removed at some later date, it might actually add to the car's value. If you are purchasing a collector car, try to purchase one with as many options as possible.

THE NON-NUMBERS-MATCHING CAR

Another decision you'll have to make is whether or not your collector car will need to have matching numbers. If so, why? Some people just don't feel right unless they own a numbers-matching car. Others intend to enter the collector car in competitions where the vehicle must be numbers-matching to be competitive.

In many cases, you can purchase an otherwise high-quality collector car at a bargain price if it is a non-numbers–matching car. If two cars are of the same year, make, and model, the numbers-matching car will be more desirable relative to the non-numbers-matching car and, therefore, more expensive.

For example, a 1970 Plymouth AAR 'Cuda that has undergone a full restoration to very high standards may be worth $65,000 if it is a numbers-matching car. The same 1970 Plymouth AAR 'Cuda, having undergone the same restoration, may only be worth $30,000 if it is a non-numbers–matching car. If it is not important to you that the numbers match, you may be able to find a bargain. Both cars should look and drive exactly the same as they travel down the road.

THE TRUE VALUE OF A COLLECTOR CAR

WHAT YOU WILL LEARN:

- What determines a car's value

- How valuable is a car to you

- The future value of collector cars

When supply is very low and demand is very high, we can expect to see an expensive collector car. Only six Bugatti Royales were built, ensuring a very low supply. Apparently, the demand is high enough to drive the value of the last Bugatti Royale to over $10,000,000 dollars. Yes, that's the right number of zeros!

There are two factors that predominantly determine a collector car's value: supply and demand, and condition.

SUPPLY AND DEMAND

First, let me illustrate how supply and demand can affect the value of a collector car. Let's start with a Bugatti Royale. Bugatti produced only six between 1929 and 1933. Apparently, the demand for this car is high relative to the supply because the last time one changed hands, it sold for over $10,000,000 dollars. Yes, that's the right number of zeros.

How about a 1948 Tucker? The Tucker Company existed just

During Tucker's one year of production, the company built only 51 cars. There are at least several hundred collectors who would like a Tucker, and therefore, they are worth in the ballpark of $500,000, although their price does fluctuate.

one year and produced only 51 cars. There are at least several hundred collectors who would like to own a Tucker, and therefore, they are in the $500,000 ballpark, although their price does fluctuate.

These are two examples of collector cars that have a low supply relative to the demand. At the other end of the spectrum, where supply is high and demand is low, one might look at the Chevrolet Vega. General Motors made almost 2,000,000 Vegas between 1971 and 1977, so clearly, they were popular during that time. Yet demand is now so low for these cars that you can practically have them for free. There was even a high-performance model called a Cosworth Vega of which only about 3,500 were produced. These are the most desirable of all Vegas, yet a low-mileage, pristine example will rarely bring more than $10,000.

Moving slightly away from these extremes are collector cars like the 1967 to 1969 Chevrolet Camaro. These cars were made in relatively large numbers, yet demand has always outpaced supply. Or the Chevrolet Corvair, for which supply has always outpaced demand. As expected, the Camaro has appreciated in value each year, and the Corvair has held steady or depreciated in value each year.

Most collector cars fall somewhere between these extremes. Here are two examples of collector cars for which the supply and demand are relatively equal. One is the Ford Mustang. The Mustang's collectible years are between mid-year-1964 and 1973. The other is the MGB, made between 1962 and 1980. Both cars were produced in large numbers—the Mustang 2,900,000 and the MGB 512,000—and both cars have had a steady demand over the years. The effect of this balance has been a relative stability in the prices, if not a slight appreciation on a yearly basis.

High supply and low demand keep prices low. There were 2,000,000 Chevrolet Vegas built during the 1970s. Only about 3,500 were Cosworth Vegas. These Vegas were powered by engines that were built by the British firm Cosworth, best known for building racing cars. The demand for these cars is so low that even a fine example costs under $10,000.00.

Even though 1967–69 Chevrolet Camaros were made in relatively large numbers, demand has always outpaced supply. Camaros, like this 1967 model, have appreciated in value each year and will most likely continue to do so as long as demand remains high.

CONDITION

The value of a collector car will often go up exponentially rather than linearly in direct relation to its condition.

Let's take a 1970 Boss 302 Mustang as an example. A parts car might be worth $10,000, while an example needing a complete restoration might be worth $20,000. A car in good usable condition may be worth $35,000, yet a Boss in very good, usable condition jumps in value to about $50,000. A high-quality car in fine condition—either restored or unrestored—might fetch $75,000, and a true show car that has been restored to the maximum professional standards and is only trailered can top $100,000. As you can see, prices can differ by 1,000% or more based solely on condition.

THE BEST VALUE FOR YOU

Does this make some collector cars better values than others? This actually depends on how you define value. Value is not spelled I-N-V-E-S-T–M-E-N-T. (This is your third warning. I promise we'll talk about investments later.) Value comprises several components, but I believe 90

percent of a collector car's value comes from the enjoyment you will receive from ownership. The other 10 percent is composed of more tangible elements, such as cost of ownership and appreciation or depreciation in value.

If you have the option of buying that $28,000 restored red Lincoln Continental convertible or a restored red Ferrari Daytona convertible for $250,000, which one represents a better value? If you like Lincolns and you don't like or can't use a Ferrari, the Lincoln is a better value for you, and it is one-tenth the price of the Ferrari!

FUTURE VALUES

Which cars are likely to gain value in the future? Nobody really knows for sure, but some general indicators have historically been correct more often than not.

One of these indicators is the average age of the population entering the collector car hobby. We can try to identify what type of car will appeal to these buyers. This is usually related to the types of cars that were popular when they were teenagers, as well as the type of car their parents owned when they were young. Sentiment is a powerful motivator when considering the purchase of a collector car.

For example, let's say the average person entering the collector car hobby in 2008 is a 45-year-old who began driving in 1979 at the age of 17. In theory, cars produced around this time should be the cars these buyers are interested in, and this is, in fact, the case for now.

We are assuming the people who are interested in these cars have the financial ability to purchase them. All the interest in the world will not increase the value of these cars without that financial ability. We may use history as a predictor, but there are no guarantees.

Another historical indicator that a car may appreciate in value is its relative rarity. In general, if a car is particularly rare, it has appreciated in value over time. However, as a collector car appreciates in value, its market diminishes. For example, just 10 years ago one could buy a very rare, high-quality, documented 1968 Shelby GT 500 Convertible for $25,000. Today that same car will sell for $250,000 or more. Naturally there are fewer buyers willing, or capable, of paying $250,000 for this car. How much higher can the price go? Nobody knows for sure.

We may also try to predict which cars will go up in value through research in much the same way an analyst might predict which stocks will go up in price. In essence, what we are trying to do is identify cars that are undervalued.

An example of this might be the 1969 1/2 Pontiac Trans Am. These cars were very rare in more ways than one. They were the only Trans

Ams produced in the original Firebird body style and were only produced for several months before Pontiac changed the body style for 1970. This led to a very limited production—only 697. The price of these cars remained steady for decades, and they could be bought for under $5,000 until the mid 1990s. Suddenly, collector car enthusiasts discovered this hidden treasure, and prices are now over $100,000 for a fine example. The few convertibles have reportedly traded for over $300,000.

Although the Chevrolet Corvair does have a dedicated following among collectors, the supply of these cars has always outpaced the demand. Prices of these cars have struggled to remain steady and may have even decreased over time. Being one subject of Ralph Nader's *Unsafe at Any Speed* has probably not helped.

MGBs, such as this 1964 model, were produced for almost two decades, and during this time, over 500,000 were built. Their sports car image combines with their simplicity to bolster demand for these cars. These factors ensure their prices will continue to appreciate modestly on a yearly basis.

Mustangs like this 1967 model were also made in large numbers. There were almost three million Mustangs produced between mid-year-1964 and 1973. Even though so many Mustangs were produced, there are a tremendous number of Mustang collectors. This large supply and larger demand has created an active market in Mustangs, and prices appreciate somewhat each year. The prices of some of the limited-production models have soared over the past few years.

There is one segment of the collector car market that has consistently increased in value and will probably continue to do so. Interestingly, this is the only segment that does not depend on the likes or dislikes of car collectors. These are the collector cars that have very low mileage and are heavily documented. They have a market value derived from these two traits. There has always been a strong demand for these cars, and I believe this trend will continue.

Collector cars are like art in that, if you are going to buy one, you must buy it because you like it. However, if you feel the uncontrollable urge to buy a collector car as an investment, this would probably be the safest segment of the market in which to invest.

THE FUTURE OF CAR COLLECTING

Let's be honest. The explosion in collector car prices that we spend a large percentage of our waking moments talking about actually applies to only a very small percentage of the collector car market. That is not to say that the market in general has not enjoyed a healthy increase in value over the past decade or so. Of course it has.

But the craziness we read about daily, such as million dollar Hemi 'Cudas (double that if you want a convertible top that goes down on a car that is never going to see the sun anyway), really only applies to a very small number of models.

The million-dollar question remains. Will this trend continue, and for how long? I, for one, believe it will. And I believe it will continue for a long, long time. How long? I'm not quite sure, but I would say at least the next 20 years. I'll give you my reasoning in a moment.

Most opinions I have read concerning value are based on one or all of the following three factors: the history of the collector car market, the financial markets in general, and the economy in general. The latter two certainly exert pressures on any market concerned with an item most rational people would consider a luxury. But car collectors are not rational, and I doubt any of us consider our collector cars luxuries.

As much as we like to think and talk about what drives the price of collector cars, it is really nothing more than the good old law of supply and demand. On the supply side, collector cars are similar to real estate in one critical way. They just ain't making any more. Actually, I would argue they stopped making any more potentially collectible cars at least 30 years ago. I'm not crazy enough to suggest there are not a few exceptions to the rule, so please don't send me any letters about your 1987 Buick GNX or your (fill in the blank). Although there are certainly peaks and valleys—no pun intended—in real estate values, over the long term, real estate will continue to increase in value. The only unknowns are how quickly and how much, but values will increase.

On the demand side, whereas they stopped making potentially collectible cars about 30 years ago, they (we) never stopped making car collectors. We humans are a pretty prolific bunch. We continue to make new people, and a certain percentage of these people are destined to become car collectors. Perhaps, they will inherit the passion for collector cars that their parents instill in them. Perhaps, they will pick it up on their own. Perhaps, it will be a nostalgia thing. Or, perhaps, it will be an

Woulda, Coulda, Shoulda

Eric had always wanted a classic Corvette. So, he bought one. It was a spur-of-the-moment decision. He saw it, he had an emotional reaction to it, and he had to have it. It was a beautiful, blue 1959 convertible.

Eric felt he deserved the Corvette. After all, he worked about 50 hours a week and had been doing so for almost 20 years. On weekends, Eric usually spent his free time with his wife Kitty and his son Michael. Sometimes, they would go camping, and sometimes, they would go on day trips. They often took along one of Michael's friends.

Have you guessed where this story is going? Eric rarely got to use his Corvette. He simply didn't have the time. On weekends, he had to choose between his Corvette and his family. OK, quiet down now! I realize it would be an easy decision for most people, but Eric chose his family.

To make matters worse, the Corvette took up the only indoor garage space in their home—a fact that did not escape his wife. Eric began to resent the car for being too small. He could have chosen to resent his family for being too big, but again, Eric chose his family over the car.

One weekend, while packing for a camping trip, Eric asked his son Michael to get the tent from the garage. A few seconds later, Eric remembered the tent was on a shelf above the Corvette. He sprinted down the stairs, through the kitchen, and into the garage, just in time to see Michael sliding the tent off of the shelf. Actually, what he was just in time to see was the six tent poles come sliding off of the shelf right onto the hood of the Corvette. Naturally, they came down pointed-end first.

Eric decided at that moment it had to go—the Corvette, not Michael—and it did. In its place, he bought a 1949 Ford Woody station wagon that he and his family loved.

Condition can affect the value of a car by 1,000%, and sometimes more. It is common for a high-quality collector car of almost any make or model to be worth ten times that of an average example of the same model. Prices of Boss 302 Mustangs, such as this 1970 model, can range from $10,000 to over $100,000, simply based on condition.

Ninety percent of a collector car's value comes from the enjoyment and use the car will provide. Regardless of its investment potential, a collector car will be of little value to you if you don't enjoy it. If you like Fords, buy a Ford. If you enjoy Ferraris, buy a Ferrari.

investment thing. Who knows? The fact remains there will always be new people entering the collector car hobby. See Barrett-Jackson's statistics for first-time attendees each year. The only unknown is, how many?

The supply side is somewhat stable because, for every car that rots away or gets wrecked, another is pulled from a barn and gets restored. The only real variable is how strong the demand will be. As I stated earlier, I believe the demand will be strong enough to maintain a healthy increase in collector car values for at least the next 20 years.

I believe the average car collector today is in his or her late-40s through early-60s. That would mean the car collectors of 20 years from now would presently be in their late-20s through early-40s. As I attend auctions, car shows, and cruise nights, I see no shortage of attendees falling within this range. Many of these people are pushing strollers and holding hands with generations of car collectors that will extend well beyond 20 years from now. If my theory is correct, much like real estate, one would expect the prices of collector cars to increase over time, with the same peaks and valleys. Historically, that is exactly what we have seen.

Will we continue to see the price of certain cars approach and even exceed $1,000,000 over the long haul? I think we will, but not with the same abandon and rapidity we have seen over the past decade. Collectors have been voracious about acquiring big-block American muscle—sometimes, with wanton abandon. How many of these cars

have we seen cross the auction block at Barrett-Jackson with questionable pedigrees, such as "re-bodies," non-matching numbers, and warranty blocks? These cars regularly sell for upwards of $500,000. Until recently, this realm was reserved only for cars with fine pedigrees and known histories.

How about big-block Corvettes and Chevelles? Are these cars really worth upwards of $250,000—sometimes way upwards? Again, it all comes down to supply and demand. I don't believe there is any shortage of supply of these cars. Everywhere you look, you see them. Today, you probably have more choice of colors and options on these cars than if you went into the dealer to buy a new one three or four decades ago. I believe that, when the market takes a close look at itself and realizes the supply of these particular cars is virtually endless, the prices may even come off a bit.

I believe we are seeing the end of an era of the meteoric rise in prices that will leave many collectors holding the proverbial bag. I think this is a grown-up game of Duck–Duck–Goose, and we will see many geese get their feathers clipped. The only collectors whose car values will stand the test of time are the ones who own cars that were truly made in very limited numbers. Virtually all Hemi-powered cars fall into this category, as do some of the L88- or L89-powered Corvettes. GTO Judges—particularly convertibles—fall into this category, as does virtually any Ram Air IV or Super Duty-powered Pontiac. Yenko & COPO Chevelles and Camaros would also join this exclusive group, as would any Stage I 455 powered Buick—especially the GSX.

We will see the more sophisticated collector turning toward the limited-production small-block cars. These would include the Boss 302 Mustang and Cougar, AAR 'Cuda, Challenger T/A, Camaro Z-28, LT-1 Corvette, and others. After all, this is a game of supply and demand, and the supply of these cars is relatively limited. I use the word sophisticated because I feel the wise investors and collectors are always on the lookout for cars with market value.

Market value can be derived from any number of sources. But I think anybody who has been involved in the collector car hobby or business for more than five minutes knows the most important factor in determining market value is rarity (production figures). How else can we explain Hemi-powered Belvederes selling for over $100,000? I realize beauty is in the eye of the beholder, but the only beautiful part of a Hemi-powered Belvedere is the part that you can't see unless you open the hood.

The market will recognize there are alternatives to big-block American muscle, and these alternatives will curry favor with collectors. We are starting to see this already. When this happens, this will reduce the demand somewhat for mega-dollar cars, and their prices will come off a bit. I believe a relatively constant demand for collector cars in general will move the prices upward. Today's $20,000 cars will become $30,000 cars; $30,000 cars will become $40,000 cars; and so on.

The other ten percent of a car's value is made up of more measurable components, such as cost of ownership and appreciation or depreciation in value. Both of these values are measurable, but not until after you've purchased the car, so both are highly speculative.

There are several factors affecting the future value of a collector car. One of these indicators is the average age of the collector and which vehicles appeal to them. Another historical indicator that a car may appreciate is its relative rarity. The early Shelbys appeal to a demographic with the financial ability to purchase one. They are also rare. These two factors have combined to escalate the price of early Shelbys.

THE LANGUAGE OF CAR COLLECTING

WHAT YOU WILL LEARN:

- The difference between frame-off and frame-on restorations

- Definitions of common car collecting terms

- The difference between original and reproduction

The term "frame-off" restoration is often used incorrectly—often referring to cars that don't even have frames. For a car to have undergone a frame-off restoration, the body must have been removed from the frame, as in this customized example.

The car collecting hobby has a language all its own, filled with specialized terms you will eventually come across in your search for a collector car. All too often, people use these terms inaccurately. People are representing cars as having undergone frame-off restorations when some of those cars don't even have frames.

Some cars have full frames, some cars have partial frames, some cars have sub-frames, and some cars don't have any frames at all. Unfortunately, the collector car

This Triumph TR4 has a "full frame" to support the body, drive train, and suspension. Later Triumphs like the TR7 and TR8 are of a "monocoque" or "unibody" construction in which the body itself provides a portion of the structural rigidity previously supplied by the frame. These cars do not have frames, yet they are often advertised as having undergone a "frame-off" restoration. Most likely, portions of the car have been disassembled in order to complete a restoration.

hobby does not have any methodology for standardizing these and many other commonly used terms. Therefore, it's the buyer's responsibility to acquire the knowledge necessary to have a clear understanding of the vehicle they are interested in purchasing.

Above: **Often when a seller describes something as "original," he means it has been restored to its original condition. If you look in the classified section of any collector car magazine, you are certain to find many advertisements starting with the words "restored original." This is an oxymoron. The dashboard of this 1965 Mustang has been restored. It is not original.**

Left: **If complete originality is of importance to you, it is best to do your homework or hire an expert before purchasing a collector car. This is the rear fin of a 1957 Chevrolet Bel Air, which opens to expose the gas cap. If you look closely, you will notice that the top spring is black and the bottom spring is silver. This is correct for this car. How many people would know that?**

This late-model Ferrari Enzo can claim to be all original. When taken within the proper context, original would be loosely defined as "exactly the way that it left the factory."

This Plymouth Duster can claim to be all original, and it is. It is important for a buyer and seller to communicate clearly exactly what original means.

FRAME-OFF VS. FRAME-ON RESTORATIONS

A frame-off restoration means the body was taken off of the chassis or frame as a part of the restoration process. A frame-on restoration means the body was not taken off of the chassis during the restoration process. These terms can be somewhat misleading and can be very subjective.

A frame-off restoration generally suggests a restoration of the highest order, whereas, a frame-on restoration indicates the restoration was completed to the highest possible standards without removing the body from the chassis. Often, you will see a collector car that has undergone a frame-on restoration that is of a higher caliber than many vehicles that have undergone frame-off restorations.

If done properly, both types of restorations are incredibly labor-intensive and are usually measured in labor hours. It is not unusual to see a collector car advertised as having undergone a 1,200-hour, frame-off restoration. Any competent shop will charge a minimum of $60 per hour for this type of work. You do the math! And this is just the labor. Don't forget to include the price of the car and the necessary parts to complete the restoration.

ORIGINAL

As applied to collector cars, the word "original" can, and often does, have many meanings. This is because when speaking of collector cars, the word does not have a specific, definable meaning unless put into a specific context.

For example, if one were to be speaking of a late-model collector car like a Ferrari Enzo or a Corvette Z06, one would expect the word original to loosely mean the car is exactly as it was when it left the factory. That is because, when put in the proper context, these cars are in new enough condition that they would not have traveled enough miles for any significant wear and tear to have taken place. Consumables, such as belts and hoses, could be expected to be

This 1966 Plymouth Satellite convertible can also claim to be original. It is not perfect, but it is in very good condition, and many collectors will pay a premium for a truly original car, even with imperfections. Many collectors use the term "survivor" to describe a car like this.

Numbers-matching means different things on different vehicles. On older Ford vehicles, the engine serial numbers generally do not match the car's vehicle identification number. This is a 1957 Ford Skyliner data plate. For this vehicle to be numbers-matching, paint color, trim, transmission, and axle must match what is on this tag.

This is the VIN tag from a 1967 Corvette. Chevrolet stamped each engine with a serial number, and the last six digits must match the last six digits of the VIN, or the car is not numbers-matching. This tag indicates the General Motors division that built the car, that it's a Corvette convertible, the manufacturing plant, and the year.

the same ones with which the car left the factory. The same would hold true for mechanical and cosmetic components. It would go without saying the vehicle in question would be roadworthy.

Not so with older collector vehicles. This is why original is so often the subject of differing opinions as to its meaning. This is also why it is so important that each vehicle must be looked at in its own individual context.

Suppose one were to find a 1931 LaSalle that had been placed in a barn when new and forgotten for the next 70 years. The vehicle remained untouched during this time, and the seller was representing this car as original. In this context, a potential buyer would have every right to reasonably assume the vehicle was still equipped with its original tires (with original air?), wires, upholstery, fluids, belts, hoses, battery, etc. The potential buyer would also expect these components would likely be so severely deteriorated as to be unusable. This might not paint a pretty picture, but because of the context, this vehicle would certainly be considered original.

Now let's look at another 1931 LaSalle that has covered only 25,000 miles in its 70+ years of existence. The present owner drives it about 500 miles per year and maintains it in a fine, roadworthy condition. The owner is selling the car and represents it as original. Once again, this is where the context of the word original becomes important.

Certainly, a reasonable potential buyer would not expect this LaSalle

Woulda, Coulda, Shoulda

Pat had finally saved enough money to buy the collector car he had dreamed of since he was a child. He began his search for a 1967 Corvette 427-435 (427-cubic-inch, 435 horsepower) coupe, and he knew he wanted a numbers-matching car. After searching in the usual places and speaking with dozens of sellers, he located one fitting all of his criteria at a dealership in Florida specializing in Corvettes.

It was a stunning Marina Blue car with a white interior that had undergone a complete, documented, frame-off restoration to National Corvette Restoration Society standards. It was well equipped and retained its original bill of sale and original tank sticker. When a Corvette was assembled, the assembly workers affixed a sticker to the top of the gas tank listing all the individual car's options. This sticker is a prized possession for the owner of any older Corvette and one of the best authentication tools a collector could be lucky enough to find. You simply can't ask for more than this in a Corvette, and it was reflected in the $100,000 price! Pat confirmed with the dealer that the engine, transmission, and rear end were all numbers-matching, and he was wise enough to have the dealer put numbers-matching on the bill of sale.

Several weeks later, an enclosed auto transporter arrived at Pat's New York home to deliver his dream car. Being that it was a Saturday afternoon, about a dozen of his neighbors came out to watch the spectacle. The transporter converted its tailgate into an elevator and lowered Pat's Corvette from the second level to street level. Pat climbed into the driver's seat and started the engine. The big 427-cubic-inch engine rumbled to life. Pat smiled and goosed the throttle a couple of times for effect. As he drove off of the ramp, applause broke out. Life was good.

Pat drove the car almost every day, and about a week after he received the car, he noticed a very small leak from one of the valve-cover gaskets. This is not a big issue nor expensive to repair. He brought it into a local shop that specialized in Corvettes. The next day Pat received a call in his office. The mechanic wanted to know if Pat was aware the cylinder heads on the engine were from a 1969 car. The mechanic informed Pat that, although the 1967 and 1969 cylinder heads were fundamentally interchangeable, the cylinder heads on his car had a date code of 1969.

Pat called the dealer in Florida and informed him of this issue, and not surprisingly, the dealer refused to do anything. The car had been sold to Pat as-is and was so indicated on the bill of sale. Pat made the argument that the bill of sale also indicated the car was numbers-matching, and the heads, which are a major component of the car, were not even from the same year car. Pat hired an attorney in Florida to pursue the matter, and after a few weeks, the dealer agreed to take the car back if Pat would ship it back at his own expense. He had already paid $1,500 to ship it from Florida to New York, and then he had to pay another $1500 to ship it back to Florida.

Fortunately, the attorney convinced the dealer it was in both parties' best interest to give Pat a $5,000 refund. This would cover most of the costs for Pat to find a set of correct date-coded cylinder heads and have them installed. It ended up costing Pat and the dealer avoidable time, money, and aggravation. On this type of car, at this price level, the definition of numbers-matching should have been clearly outlined in the bill of sale.

This outcome is the best Pat could have hoped for. He had to pay an attorney several hundred dollars, lost the use of his car while new cylinder heads were sourced and installed, and had a bit of aggravation.

to have its original tires, battery, spark plugs, belts, or hoses. If it did, it would not be roadworthy. The potential buyer knows this car is in fine, roadworthy condition, and the potential buyer should have some pre-conceived notion of what the word original means in this context.

So, what does the word original actually mean when used in this context? It's hard to say exactly because there are so many variables, such as age, mileage, maintenance, and storage conditions. In this instance, I would presume original might loosely be defined the following way: substantially unmodified and consisting of the major components with which the vehicle left the factory. Ordinary wear and tear would be expected, as would replacement of consumables necessary to keep the vehicle in fine, roadworthy condition.

Original does not have specific definable meaning without a specific context. Even when put

Numbers-matching can, and often does, extend to major components other than the engine. This is a Chevrolet four-speed transmission with the serial number stamped into the casing.

into a specific context, the buyer and seller must agree to a specific meaning.

NUMBERS-MATCHING

Numbers-matching means different things when applied to different vehicles. In its purest sense, it means certain components of a vehicle, which serial numbers or codes identify, are the original components for that individual vehicle. These components include engines, transmissions, and differential housings.

Ambiguity arises because different manufacturers assigned codes in different manners. For example, some manufacturers included a portion of the vehicle identification number in the serial numbers of major components of the car. Other manufacturers only put date codes on these major components, and therefore, they were never intended to match the VIN of that particular car. Therefore, the term "numbers-

This VIN tag is not original. For some reason, the original VIN tag is gone. In most states, it is illegal to modify or remove a VIN tag. In this case, the State of Nevada has issued its own VIN tag to replace the original. Any time a VIN tag has been removed, even if it has been replaced, the vehicle's provenance is questionable.

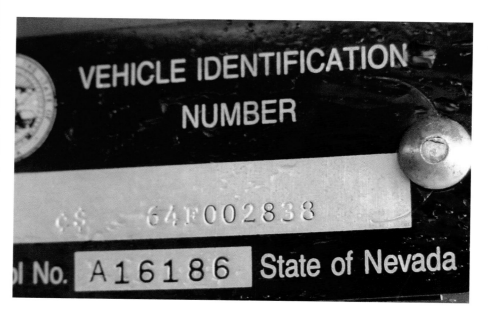

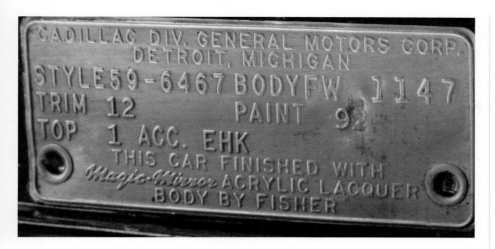

This is a 1959 Cadillac data plate. If you look closely at the two-digit code next to the word "paint," the second digit in the paint code has been made illegible. There is no way to be absolutely certain what color this car was when it left the factory.

matching" derives its definition as it applies to a specific vehicle.

The term numbers-matching is very important to understand before you purchase a collector car because it will have a significant impact on the value of the car. If the seller represents the car as being numbers-matching, make sure you and the seller agree on exactly what numbers match.

Many sellers represent a car as numbers-matching simply because it was represented to them when they purchased it, and they have never verified it. Some sellers consider a car to be numbers-matching if the engine is the correct engine for that vehicle. Others consider a car to be numbers-matching if the engine, transmission, and differential housing are correct for that vehicle. I tend to agree with this definition. Still others will insist that all of the numbers have to be correct, including cylinder heads, distributors, carburetors, water pumps, and manifolds.

As a general rule, within a specific make and model, the more expensive the car, the more numbers should match. For example, a numbers-matching 1963 Corvette

that is being offered for $60,000 should have its original engine, transmission, and differential housing. The same 1963 Corvette that is selling for $100,000 should have all of the correct numbers on components like cylinder heads, distributor, carburetor, water pump, manifolds, and more.

If you are buying a collector car represented as numbers-matching, it is imperative you verify this. Inform the seller that you expect him or her to show you these numbers no matter how inconvenient it may be. On some vehicles, this is relatively easy and may be done right on the spot. On other collector cars, the numbers will have to be recorded and researched. If the seller is unable to do this, hire an inspector. This is often labor-intensive and can cost hundreds of dollars, but it is money well spent.

Presumably, if a car is represented as numbers-matching, it will reflect in the price. I can't tell you how many collector cars I've seen that the owners believed were numbers-matching and were not. The time to discover this is before you purchase the car!

Date-coding is one method to determine if a component might be original to a specific car. If this power steering box, which was manufactured on July 24, 1968, turns up on a 1967 car, you can be certain the power steering box was not originally installed on that car.

DATE CODES AND CASTING CODES

Date-coding tells when a particular component was manufactured. Sometimes, this can only be accurate to within a particular month of a particular year. Other times, it can be accurate to the exact date. Most manufacturers date-coded a significant number of parts on a car. These parts include the block, cylinder heads, intake and exhaust manifolds, carburetor, distributor, transmission, differential housing, alternator, and water pump. These date codes help determine if these components might have been original to a specific collector car.

On cars that are date-coded well, it is possible to determine with certainty if an individual component is not original to a specific car. Unfortunately, the reverse is not true. It is not possible to say with certainty that an individual component is original to a specific car. For example, in almost all collector cars, the engine's build date precedes the car's build date because most engines were built in a different factory than the cars for which they were destined. The factory shipped the engine in advance to the car assembly plant to await installation into a particular vehicle as it came down the assembly line.

If we inspect a collector car and determine the engine was built after the car, we can say with almost absolute certainty that it is not the car's original engine. If, however, we inspect a car and determine the engine was built several months before the car itself, then we can only say this might be the original engine that came in this car. The only way to determine if it is, in fact, the original engine that came in the car is if the manufacturer stamped a serial number on the engine that matches the car's VIN. Some manufacturers did this, and some did not.

Cast-coding communicates more information from many components of a collector car. As its name implies, cast-coding applies only to parts cast out of iron, aluminum, or other metals. Cast-coding contains information

Most manufacturers put cast codes on major components containing many different types of information. In this case, the block code 9778789 indicates this Pontiac engine was used in a 1965 or 1966 vehicle. The engine produced between 256 and 360 horsepower. The date code below the block code further indicates this block was cast on February 20, 1965.

relevant to that specific part, such as place of manufacture and intended application. The importance of cast codes is similar to that of date codes. These codes may also be used to determine if a particular part may have been original to a specific car.

Once again, you can only determine with certainty that it was not. You cannot use cast-coding to determine if it was original. For example, the Chevrolet 350-cubic-inch engine is probably the most common engine in the world today. They are easily interchangeable from one car to the next. Yet Chevrolet has put a cast code on each and every block to identify what its intended application was. If a 350-cubic-inch engine has a cast code indicating its application was for a truck with an automatic transmission, and it turns up in a Corvette with a four-speed transmission, you can be certain this engine was not the original installed in the car at the factory. However, if the cast code does in fact indicate that its intended application was a Corvette with a four-speed transmission, you still can't be certain this is the original engine. Once again, if available, we need to turn to a serial number on the engine that matches the vehicle's VIN.

NOS, NORS, AND REPRODUCTION PARTS

When the need arises to replace a part on a collector car, the source of that part can potentially become important, depending on the originality of the collector car as well as your desire to maintain that level of originality.

NOS means New Old Stock. This sounds like an oxymoron, but in fact, it is the Holy Grail of replacement parts. An NOS part is one the original manufacturer produced at the time it was needed in order to manufacture a particular car. It would likely have been in the parts department of a new car dealership or distribution center. It would not have been available in an auto parts store.

NORS means New Old Replacement Stock. An NORS part may or may not have been manufactured by the original part manufacturer. It, too, may have been in the parts department of a new car dealership or distribution center. It may also have been in an auto parts store.

Reproduction means exactly that. The part has been reproduced, often in response to a large demand from the collector car market. Reproduction parts are very popular and very common on collector cars. They are generally significantly less expensive than comparable NOS or

Sometimes cast codes, which may include date codes, can have a significant impact on the value of a part. The blue "round port" cylinder heads shown here are very rare and very difficult to find. Even in their present unrestored condition, the seller is asking $3,500.

NORS parts. They are also subject to wide variations in quality. For example, reproduction body parts are often dimensionally different from the original parts they are intended to replace.

Recently, some of the major manufacturers, such as General Motors, have begun licensing the rights to reproduce original General Motors parts for the collector car hobby. The parts are generally of a very high quality, and they are often indistinguishable from the originals.

CLONES

A clone is a collector car built or restored to be an exact duplicate of another specific collector car. It is generally a duplicate of a very desirable, expensive, or limited-production vehicle. A clone uses the same type of chassis and body as the original and usually has the identical drivetrain, interior, and exterior markings. The more accurately a clone duplicates the original, the higher the value of the clone.

For example, Chevrolet built a handful of high-performance

Camaros in 1969 identified as COPO (Central Office Processing Order) in their VINs. These are extremely rare and highly sought after. Prices for a high-quality COPO Camaro are well over $100,000. Someone who enjoys the look and uniqueness of this car can reproduce the car for about one third that price. The original COPO Camaro and the clone may appear absolutely identical to all but those with an expertise in the field of COPO Camaros.

Herein lies the danger. Whereas most people involved in the collector car hobby or business are honest, there are those who are not, and they may represent a clone as the real deal.

Once again, as in buying a non-numbers-matching collector car, purchasing a clone might be right for you. As long as you are aware it is a clone. It is like buying costume jewelry. Only you'll know for sure.

In 1970, Chevrolet produced a very limited number of Chevelle Super Sports equipped with a 454-cubic-inch engine called an LS6.

Cast codes are typically used on items like engine blocks, cylinder heads, intake manifolds, exhaust manifolds, and other cast-iron parts. If an item contains only cast codes and no serial numbers, they can be replaced, and the car will still be considered original. Many items look identical and are interchangeable, so it is critical to be certain the cast codes are correct.

These are extremely rare and, due to their 450-horsepower rating, very desirable. There is a joke perpetually circulating among car collectors that, on any given day, you can find more 1970 Chevelle Super Sports with LS6 engines advertised than Chevrolet ever produced, and you can be sure they are not all represented as clones.

REPRODUCTION CARS

A reproduction car is one intended to resemble as closely as possible another very desirable car at less cost. The components needed to assemble reproduction cars are usually mass-produced. Either a factory assembles them, or they may be purchased in kit form for the customer to assemble. They generally

The cast code visible on this Chrysler engine is 2536430-10, which indicates it is a 440-cubic-inch 4-barrel V-8 produced between 1966 and 1972. To further refine the date, we would need to locate the date code. If this engine appears in a 1970 Plymouth Roadrunner, we can be certain it is not the original engine because 1970 Roadrunners were only available with 383-cubic-inch engines, 440 6-Pack engines, and 426 Hemi engines.

NOS means New Old Stock. This might sound like an oxymoron, but it is not. It is actually a new part. However, it is also an old part because it was manufactured many years ago. It would usually have been in a dealer's stock. It will have correct codes if applicable. Often, an NOS part is in its original box like this tachometer drive gear.

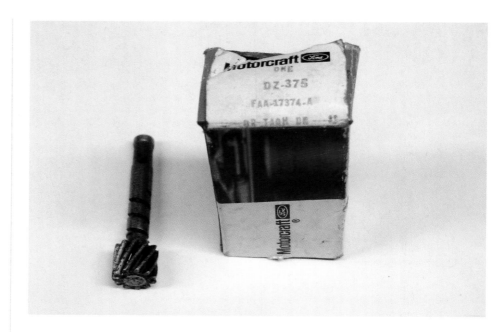

do not have exactly the same type of chassis or drivetrain as the original car. Often, the body is not made of the same material as the original car, and the interiors often are not the same.

Reproduction cars vary greatly in their construction methods, quality, and materials. If it is very desirable, there are often several companies making reproductions of the same model of car. For example, there are at least ten companies making reproductions of the AC Cobra. Most of these companies manufacture their own chassis. Some companies sell these as complete cars and others sell them as kits. There are several body styles available with dozens of options and unlimited powertrain choices. Some are made of steel and some of fiberglass. The quality of these cars differs significantly as

NORS means New Old Replacement Stock. An NORS part may or may not have been manufactured by the original part manufacturer. It, too, may have been in the parts department of a new car dealership or distribution center. It may also have been in an auto parts store.

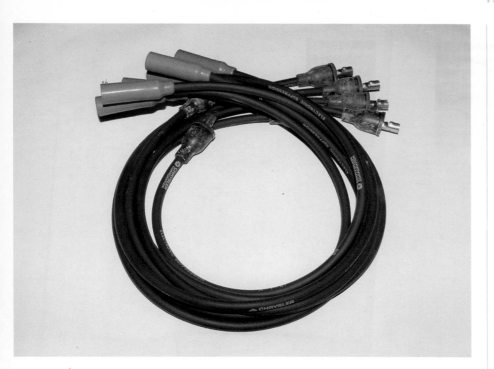

Reproduction parts are common on collector cars. They are generally less expensive than comparable NOS or NORS parts. They are also subject to variations in quality. Recently, some of the major manufacturers, such as General Motors, have begun licensing the rights to reproduce original General Motors parts for the collector car hobby. These parts are generally of a very high quality. Often, they are indistinguishable from the original parts they are intended to replace.

does the price, which can range from as low as $20,000 to as high as $100,000 or more.

There are several models of reproduction Ferraris. The Daytona Spyder convertible reproduction is usually built on a Chevrolet Corvette chassis and may or may not have an accurate Ferrari interior. The Testarossa reproduction is usually on a Pontiac Fiero chassis and usually utilizes the original Fiero interior.

Reproduction car builders often use as many of the parts from the original car as is economically possible. This can often cost thousands or tens of thousands of dollars. The number of original parts, coupled with the quality of the finished product, will determine the value of the reproduction car.

Regardless of the cost or quality of a reproduction car, they rarely increase in value because they are not real. They are simply copies of other cars. Their market value is nothing more than the cost of parts and labor, which is then depreciated over time as the market sees fit. This depreciation time can be very short. It is not at all unusual to see these

These reproduction ignition wires were manufactured under license from Chrysler Corporation. If you look closely, you will see they contain the date code "1–67." This means they are reproductions of ignition wires produced in January of 1967. Attention to this kind of detail is important if you want to complete a faithful restoration to original factory specifications.

Some clones are so well built, they are virtually impossible to distinguish from the original. The more original parts that are used, and the more attention to detail, the more valuable the clone will be. Although immaculate in appearance, this Yenko Camaro clone engine differs from the original in many details. Note the "Yenko SC 427" decal on the radiator shroud, which has been added to increase the appearance of authenticity.

cars sell for fifty cents on the dollar just days after they are completed.

ORPHAN CARS

As the name suggests, an orphan car is one left behind by its parent—parent company, that is—due to any number of causes. Perhaps, the parent company couldn't sell enough cars to make a profit, or perhaps, their styling was questionable at the time, but for whatever reason, they are no longer in business. The term "orphan car" also extends to discontinued divisions of companies that still exist. One example would be DeSoto, which was a division of Chrysler.

As a subset of the collector car hobby, orphan cars exhibit the same diversity as any other type of collector car. Orphan cars range from the somewhat obscure, such as Moon, Muntz Jet, and Terraplane, to some of the most

recognizable and expensive, such as Auburn, Duesenberg, and Tucker.

Other common examples are Edsel, Hudson, Nash, Packard, Studebaker, Hupmobile, Essex, Cord, Willys, Pierce Arrow, and Thomas Flyer. Two recent examples are Bricklin and DeLorean.

Orphan car owners make up some of the closest-knit communities within the collector car hobby because most of these manufacturers have been out of business for a long time, eliminating a direct source of parts and information. Owners of these cars depend on a network of other owners to keep their cars on the road.

UNDERVALUED CARS

I define an undervalued car as a collector car that, when viewed on its own merits, should garner much more attention than it actually does.

These cars should have distinguished themselves for styling,

If you're in the market for something small, fast, and flashy, a nice 1969 Corvette or Camaro will cost upwards of $30,000—sometimes way upwards. "Orphan cars" like this 1982 DeLorean can be a great bargain in the collector car market. This DeLorean will perform with the best of these at a fraction of the cost. Best of all, you won't see one at every show!

performance, or limited production but, for some reason, have not. Some undervalued cars do get discovered and become very collectible, enjoying a rapid increase in value. An example would be the 1968 through 1970 AMC AMX and the mid-year-1969 Pontiac Trans Am. As little as five years ago, $25,000 could purchase a fine 1969 1/2 Trans-Am. As of this writing, the price is well over $100,000.

Here are some examples of cars I consider undervalued. One of my favorites is the 1956 and 1957 Lincoln Continental Mark II. Ford virtually hand-built these beautiful cars and lost $1,000 on each car. Fortunately, Ford only produced 2,550 in 1956 and 444 in 1957. Ford priced them at over $10,000— a hefty sum in those days, and twice the price of any other new Lincoln. Today, less than $40,000 can buy a fine example.

Jumping ahead two decades, we find another undervalued car— the 1977 Pontiac Can Am. Pontiac produced only 1,130 examples. Until very recently, many collectors considered the styling questionable. However, as the demographics show, the Baby Boomers who now buy collector cars came of age around 1977, and these are the cars they remember. Today, a high-quality Can Am costs less than $15,000.

Just before Pontiac produced the Can Am, Chevrolet produced its own car destined to remain undervalued—the Cosworth Vega. In 1975 and 1976, Chevrolet only produced approximately 3,500 of these special models. In comparison, Chevrolet produced 2,000,000 Vegas during its entire production run. Cosworths had a graphics package that set it apart from anything else on the road, but what really made it special was its high-performance, twin-cam engine, which was a collaboration between Chevrolet and Cosworth of England. Today, a very-high-quality example costs under $10,000.

Reproduction cars are intended to replicate another vehicle cosmetically, not mechanically. They often have a modern, dependable drivetrain and chassis. These cars may sometimes be built by a factory, but often they are sold as kits. Detail and quality of materials varies greatly, as do the prices. The Auburn boat-tail speedster is one of the more popular reproduction cars.

THE PROS AND CONS OF RESTORATION

Chapter 4

WHAT YOU WILL LEARN:

• The true cost of restoration

• The Golden Rule

• Exceptions to the Rule

Buying a collector car that has undergone a recent full restoration can often turn out to be a bargain. Rarely can the costs of a restoration be recovered without waiting for the car to appreciate in value. A full restoration of a car like this Pontiac GTO might cost $50,000 or more, yet you can purchase the same car after a recent restoration for $25,000.

Buying a recently restored collector car can often turn out to be a real bargain. Chances are very good the seller will lose a lot of money, and you will save a lot of money. Restorations are very expensive, often totaling significantly more than the car is worth. If the seller has to sell this car before its value has had a chance to appreciate, it will sell at a loss with few exceptions.

COST CONSIDERATIONS

I can't forbid you from buying a car that needs restoration, but if I could, I would. As I promised earlier, I'll explain this in a little more detail. Naturally, the market for different cars varies, however, the principle I am going to demonstrate applies to most collector cars. We'll start by introducing a few new words and phrases here that are

common to the collector car hobby. Don't be scared. There are definitions at the back of this book with simple explanations for any words that you don't understand.

Before we start, let's make two assumptions. The first assumption is that your budget for a completed car is $28,000. The second assumption is that you don't want to do, or are not capable of doing, the work yourself.

Let's go back to that shiny red Lincoln convertible you've decided to buy, and let's say you've found two for sale. They differ somewhat in condition and price, as well as location. The lower-priced one is in poorer shape and needs to be restored, but it is local. The more expensive one is fully restored, but it is 1,500 miles away in sunny Arizona.

Let's take a simple look at the financial considerations of restoring the local Lincoln compared to buying the fully restored Lincoln in Arizona. The owner of the Lincoln 1,500 miles from home tells you the car is fully restored. It is not a frame-off restoration but, rather, a frame-on restoration of a numbers-matching,

This car has been stripped to the bare metal and then primed and finished in a high-quality base-coat/clear-coat paint. This can easily cost $10,000. Most of the chrome has been re-plated, and the stainless-steel pieces were polished. Re-plating all the chrome pieces, including the bumpers, will cost approximately $2,500.

The convertible top has been replaced with a new top of the type with which the car originally left the factory. At the same time, the convertible top frame was refinished. The cost for this, including rear window, top pads, and new boot, was $2,200.

The leather seats and door panels have been recovered in the proper patterns and with the proper materials. The carpet has also been replaced.
The total cost for these items, including materials and labor, is $8,500.

rust-free Arizona car. He's even had the Lincoln and Continental Owners Club document it.

The car has been stripped to bare metal. There was very little rust, and in the few areas that rust did exist, patch panels were welded in place. The seller re-plated most of the chrome and polished the stainless steel, and he then primed and finished the car in a high-quality, base-coat/clear-coat paint.

The seller replaced the convertible top with a new original-type top and recovered the seats and door panels with proper leather and trim, and he replaced the carpet. He got the air conditioning working and repaired a few faulty gauges.

The proud seller rebuilt the engine, transmission, front end, and brakes, and he installed a new exhaust system. Everything now works, including the power windows, power top, and vacuum-operated power door locks. The car has new tires, a fresh tune-up, and an oil change.

The seller has receipts for all the work, and he has owned the car for 15 years. He claims you could get into this car and drive the 1,500 miles to your house. He wants $28,000 for the car, which happens to be exactly what you have budgeted.

Unfortunately, it's also going to cost you $1,000 to have the car transported to your home. You

THE PROS AND CONS OF RESTORATION

decide to have the car checked out and contact an inspector in his hometown. The inspector sends you a report, and the car is exactly the way the owner represented it.

While that seems like a good deal, you start thinking about the fact that the owner of the local Lincoln only wants $7,000 for his car. However, it really does need a complete restoration to be dependable and present the appearance that you wish. It will need the same type of restoration the Arizona Lincoln went through.

The good news is, after paying only $7,000 for the car, you'll still have $21,000 left for the restoration. Surely, you can replicate the Arizona Lincoln's restoration for $21,000. After all, your parents didn't even pay $21,000 for their house! I'm not really sure how that applies here, but it's an argument I hear with relative frequency when discussing the cost of restorations. You decide to put some rough numbers down on paper to prove to yourself what a financial genius you are and to figure out what you're going to do with all the money that's left over.

First, you decide to visit your local restoration shop to see if you can get some accurate prices. The first thing you find out is there is no local restoration shop. There is a shop that will do the paint job and all of the associated work, but they don't do convertible tops, interiors, engines, or transmissions. You'll have to pick up all of your chrome pieces as soon as they are removed and send them out yourself for re-plating, but not to worry, they know somebody with a truck who will deliver them to you, which is great,

The engine and transmission were removed, rebuilt, detailed, and reinstalled at a cost of $5,700. At the same time, the engine bay was detailed to original factory specifications.

The air conditioning has been made functional, and a few of the gauges that didn't work were repaired. The front end has been rebuilt, and the brake system has been completely replaced, as has the exhaust. The exhaust will cost $800, the front end $900, and the entire brake system will run $1,200.

The trunk area has been detailed to original factory specifications. This includes carpeting, spare tire cover, hard trim covering, taillight wiring, jack hold-downs, and pouches.

since they weigh 200 pounds and won't fit in your Volkswagen Jetta.

Your next stop is the local engine rebuilder that was recommended to you, but he doesn't do transmissions. He recommends his brother-in-law, who will rebuild your transmission in his garage after work—maybe, maybe not.

Now, it's off to the upholstery shop. This must be your lucky day.

They also install convertible tops and carpeting. The exhaust shop can handle the brakes and the front end, and they happen to know somebody who can repair the power windows, gauges, door locks, and air conditioning, and make the power top go up and down again. You head over there to get these final prices, and now, you are on your way home to add them all up.

Everything now works, including the power windows, power top, and power door locks. It cost $4,500 to repair or replace these items. These systems are complicated, parts are scarce, and the experts charge a premium.

HERE IS WHAT YOU FIND:

Paint and bodywork:	$9,500
Re-plating of chrome parts	$2,500
Interior (including seats, door panels, and carpeting)	$8,500
Convertible top (including rear window)	$2,200
Engine rebuild	$4,500
Transmission rebuild	$1,200
Exhaust	$800
Front end	$900
Brake system	$1,200
Power windows, gauges, door locks, air conditioning, and power top	$4,500

Your heart sinks a little as you realize, so far, you're up to $35,800, and that does not even include the $7,000 for the car! At this point, another thought keeps running through your mind: Everybody you visited, from the body shop to the engine rebuilder, warned you their price could go up significantly depending on what they found once they got started.

In the back of your mind, you were also kind of wondering how you would get a car that was in pieces from one shop to another. At this point, you most likely hadn't even considered the fact that the restoration you were anticipating would take years to complete. So, you didn't worry about new tires, tune-up, and an oil change.

Any literature or records pertaining to a specific vehicle will enhance its provenance. Prior registrations, insurance cards, or the original factory invoice can verify its history.

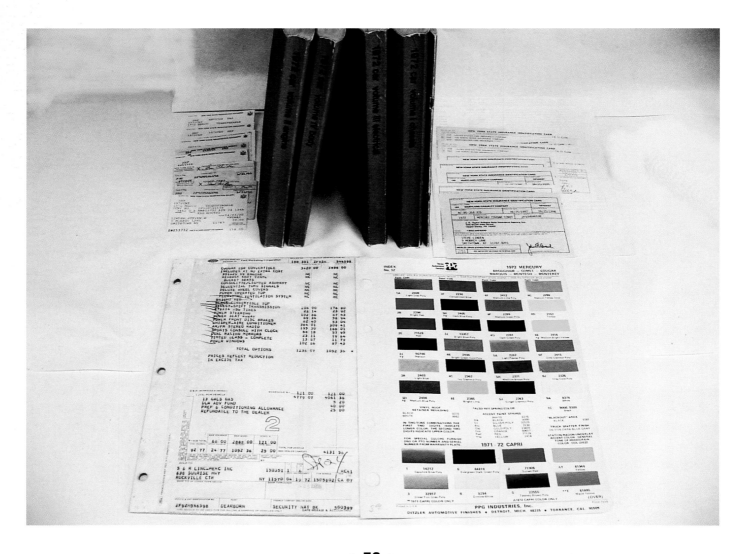

So, we find ourselves wondering why the owner of the Lincoln in Arizona is willing to sell his car for only $28,000. This is the easiest question of all to answer. The answer is—drum roll, please—because that's what it's worth.

Remember, two factors determined the value of a collector car—supply and demand and condition. Although Lincoln Continental convertibles are wonderful cars,

there is a relatively generous supply and a relatively limited demand. This limits the price that they will sell for on the open market.

THE RULE

The Golden Rule in the collector car hobby is, "You cannot restore a collector for less than the cost of buying a car that is already restored." If there is one rule to memorize, this is it! There are a few exceptions in

In theory, it is possible to make money restoring collector cars. You will need a combination of desire, skill, and property to store parts-cars. If you concentrate on one particular series of one particular model of one particular manufacturer, such as these MGs, it might just work.

If you own a body shop, you already have the labor force to do the cosmetics. This kind of work is not nearly as profitable as the collision work you normally do. However, when your shop is not busy, you can find a relatively nice car you can paint and resell, hopefully for a profit.

If you have a large sum of money and insist on investing in something risky, buy a few classic cars, rent a shop, hire a mechanic, do a little work on each, and try selling them at a profit. Beware: one mistake can be very expensive. This small amount of coolant was a clue that the original block on this car was cracked and needed to be replaced, diminishing the value of the car by thousands of dollars.

which it does make sense to restore a collectible car. Most do not make sense for the average collector. Read through them yourself, and see if they apply to you.

EXCEPTIONS TO THE RULE

Exception #1

You started restoring cars 25 years ago and decided you really enjoyed restoring 1967 through 1969 Chevrolet Camaros. Many years and many thousands of dollars later, you discovered you could buy completely restored cars for less money than it was costing you to restore them. But you really loved restoring 1967–1969 Camaros. It was your true calling in life, and you had a plan.

So, with the blessing of your very understanding wife and family, you sold your nice house with the swimming pool and bought a piece

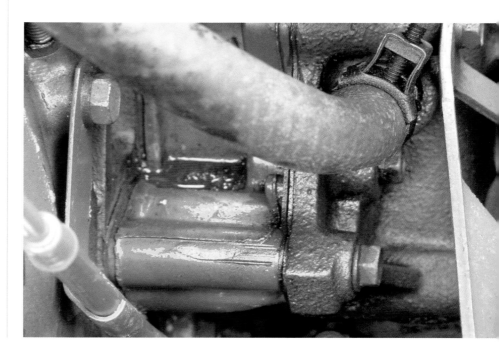

of property 20 miles outside of town with a big empty lot out back (no zoning laws, this is critical), and plenty of room to store cars and parts. You started accumulating parts cars you had no intention of ever restoring but, rather, would be an inexpensive source of parts. The labor you would do yourself. You had inadvertently discovered that, if you were willing to dedicate you life to the pursuit of restoring one particular series of one particular model of one particular manufacturer, you could probably make a living doing this. That is, assuming you have the requisite diverse skills to do the work yourself. You have discovered one of the few exceptions to the Golden Rule. Does this sound like you?

Exception #2

You own a body shop that is not busy all the time. Some of your employees are standing around looking for something to do. You have two choices: You can fire people when there is no work, or you can have these employees randomly push cars into the middle of the street in hopes of drumming up business. Neither option appeals to you, so you decide to buy a collector car as a shop project for the times the shop isn't busy.

You find a relatively nice car you can paint and resell, and make a few bucks. You really can't restore it because if you have to farm out any work, such as the upholstery or engine, you won't make any money.

Buy low, sell high! Easier said than done. The buying part is easy. It's the selling part that's hard. Collector cars may be undervalued for any number of reasons. Season, location, or the seller's need to dispose of the car quickly may affect prices. You could buy Porsche Speedster convertibles during a Northeast winter and sell them in Southern California where they are more highly valued.

If you don't have the funds to buy a restored car, you can restore one over a period of time. Mustangs are excellent candidates for restoration. They are easy to work on, and parts are readily available and inexpensive. When the restoration is complete, it is likely you will have spent more money than the car is worth. However, this has enabled you to complete a restoration within a workable financial framework.

This is an ideal situation for you because you have the labor to complete the work. You have to pay them whether they work or not. You will probably be able to sell the car and recover the cost of your labor. The best part is that you didn't have to fire anybody, and thankfully, the shop is busy again with collision work with which you actually make money. You realize that this shop project is only for quiet times, and you won't really make any money, but rather, you will just cover payroll. You have discovered another exception to the Golden Rule. How about it? Does this sound like you?

Exception #3

You've just taken an early retirement package from your company, and you have a large sum of money to invest. You no longer have a job. This is a critical requirement because your new venture will occupy you full time. You've also decided you really don't want to do something safe with the money. After all, your parents didn't pay for your college, so why should you pay for your kid's college? And you love collector cars.

So you decide you are going to buy a few of these cars, rent a shop, hire a mechanic or two, do a little work on each and try to resell them at a profit. Your job will be to travel around the country (remember, you came into a large sum of money) and find just the right cars and ship them back to your shop. There, your mechanics will do just a little bit of work on each to add value, and you will sell these cars at a substantial profit.

Of course, we'll assume you know just which cars are the right cars. We'll also assume you have a thorough mechanical knowledge of these cars, not to mention you know how to make sure the numbers match on all of these cars because one mistake could cost you tens of thousands of dollars. If you meet all of these

In most cases, it will cost just as much money to restore a very desirable car as it will to restore a less desirable car. Take this into account if you believe you will be selling this car at some time in the near future. Otherwise, somebody else will be the beneficiary of your hard work and financial investment. Corvettes are one of the most popular candidates for restoration because of their wide appeal.

criteria, you just might be able to make some money.

After all, other people are in fact doing it. They're very easy to spot at the large shows. They're the ones who are sleeping in $500,000 motor homes. Parked right behind their motor homes are their car transporters, which can carry up to eight cars. Does economy of scale ring a bell? They arrived at the show a day early, and by 6:00 a.m. on the opening day of the show, they had already purchased the five most desirable cars. The mechanics that they had brought along had inspected the cars right on the spot. They had found another one of the few exceptions to the Golden Rule. Does this sound like you?

Exception #4

This is the exception to invoke if you have a significant amount of money to invest (risk) in a collector car venture, and perhaps, you wish to maintain another job, which is probably a very good idea.

It is called buy low/sell high. You may have heard of this, as it sometimes applies to commodities other than collector cars. It is quite simple in theory. Find cars you feel are undervalued—hoping you are right—buy them, and sell them at a higher price.

Collector cars may be undervalued for any number of reasons. There is always a source of cars available at wholesale prices—yes, even collector cars—if you can tap into this source. Another thing that affects the values of collector cars in many parts of this country is the season. For example, it is much more difficult to sell a collector car during a snowstorm in the Northeast, and prices reflect this. A car may be undervalued relative to where it is located. Perhaps you could buy several Volkswagen Karmann Ghia convertibles on the

Woulda, Coulda, Shoulda

About two years ago, Bill's friend was selling a 1957 Jaguar XK-150 coupe for the seemingly low price of $2,500. It had been sitting unused in his friend's damp garage for as long as Bill could remember—at least ten years. Bill had admired the classic lines of this British sports car every time he had seen it, and he thought that, for only $2,500, this would be his golden opportunity to get into the collector car hobby. And what better way to start than with a Jaguar?

So he bought it, and he called me to come take a look at it. The car was complete, and from ten feet away it looked decent, but it quickly became obvious it was in need of a total restoration. Signs of exterior rust were visible, leaving one to wonder what wasn't visible. The interior was dried and cracked, and mice had pulled all the stuffing out of the seats, as well as having consumed the insulation off the cloth-covered wiring harnesses. The oil on the dipstick showed signs of water contamination, which (combined with the fact it hadn't been started in ten years) would mean tearing down the engine and rebuilding it. I didn't even bend down to look underneath the car.

"Sell it or give it away, it doesn't matter. Even if you give it away, you've only lost your $2,500. If you restore it, you're going to lose a lot more." That was my advice to Bill, who stared at me in disbelief. I explained to Bill that, after a restoration to high standards, the car would only be worth $50,000 on a good day. A restoration to these standards could easily exceed $100,000 at a reputable, well-known shop. As luck would have it, there was a well-known Jaguar specialty shop less than twenty miles from Bill's home.

Bill visited the shop, and they informed him a proper restoration would take between 500 and 1000 hours at $100 per hour. This did not include parts. He decided to proceed with the restoration.

Why did he make this decision? I can't answer that, but I can tell you people make similar decisions every day. Look in any collector car publication, and you'll find numerous ads for vehicles being sold for half or less than what's been invested in them. In fact, there are so many people who make this mistake that a term has evolved to describe this situation. When an owner has more money invested in a collector car than it's worth, it's called being under water.

Fast-forward two years to the present day. The restoration has been completed to very high standards. The credentials of the shop that performed the work are impeccable. Receipts have been retained, and the complete restoration has been documented with photographs. Acceptable modifications have been performed to the brakes and cooling system to make the car usable in today's environment.

All together, Bill has invested almost $150,000, not including the cost of the car. He now wishes to sell the car. So far, he has been unable to sell it for $60,000. He's just lowered the price to $50,000. Why? Because that's what it's worth.

This true story can be positive or negative. It's clearly negative if you're Bill. However, if you're in the market for a Jaguar XK-150 coupe, it could be very positive.

If you remember the Golden Rule of the collector car hobby, which is that you cannot restore a collector for less than the cost of buying a car that is already restored, you'll be viewing this story in a very positive light.

No matter how much time and money you invest restoring a car, it will only be worth what the market will bear. A fully restored AMC Gremlin may only be worth $4,000 even after an extensive restoration, but a 1970 AMC AMX may be worth $25,000 after a comparable restoration costing the same amount of money.

East Coast and ship them to southern California, where they are much more desirable. Or maybe you know of someone who has a collection of cars for sale you can buy at a significant discount if you agree to buy them all. You could break up the collection and realize the profit in that way. There are many different ways to buy collector cars at discounts, and Exception #4 applies to all of them.

Exception #5

There is one instance where restoring a collector car does make sense. It makes sense if you take the financial factor out of the equation. Suppose you don't have $30,000 to buy the collector car of your dreams, but you do have $10,000, and you will have $1,000 per month to invest in the restoration. By the time you have completed the restoration, you will probably have

invested $50,000 to restore a collector car with a value of $30,000. From a purely financial perspective, this does not make sense. However, this has enabled you to complete a restoration within a financial framework you are comfortable with, and you now own the collector car of your dreams.

WHAT TYPE OF CAR TO RESTORE

Ask yourself the same three questions you would be asking yourself if you were buying a completely restored collector car. What do you like? What are you going to use it for? How much do you want to spend? Once you've answered these questions, you will know what kind of collector car to restore.

However, there are some additional issues to consider. Most importantly, remember that, in most cases, it will cost just as much to restore a very desirable car as it

Some restorations can be very expensive simply because parts are very difficult to find. These parts are said to be made of "unobtainium." Some cars, such as the Boss 302 Mustang have several parts that are extremely difficult to find—the smog pump and rev limiter, for example. The rev limiter is the small rectangular box at the top-center of this photo.

will to restore a less desirable car. You should take this into account if you believe you will sell this collector car in the future.

Example: Assume your budget is $25,000 to purchase and restore a collector car. You could purchase a 1978 AMC Pacer for $1,000 in need of complete restoration. Or you could purchase a 1969 Chevrolet Camaro for $5,000 in need of complete restoration. You will then spend approximately $20,000 on either car to have it restored to an acceptable level. This would include having the car painted, having the interior reupholstered, replacing the chrome and stainless items, and performing all of the mechanical work necessary to make the car 100 percent functional. When all of this work is done, you

will have an AMC Pacer that may be worth $4,000 or a Chevrolet Camaro that may be worth $25,000. Either way, the investment in the restoration will cost just about the same amount for either collector car.

Naturally, there are exceptions to this rule—predominantly collector cars for which parts are very scarce. For example, it would certainly cost more money to restore a 1969 Boss 302 Mustang fastback than a 1969 base-model 302 Mustang fastback. Certain parts necessary for the Boss 302 restoration are very hard to find and are, therefore, very expensive. These expensive items include smog pumps and rev limiters. Other than the cost of these and other scarce items, the cost of the restoration should be identical.

A basic restoration to high-quality driver standards would include having the car painted, having the interior reupholstered, replacing the chrome, and performing all the mechanical work necessary to make the car 100 percent functional. This restoration may cost $25,000 or more, depending on the condition and complexity of the car, as well as availability of parts.

FIND YOUR DREAM CAR

Chapter 5

WHAT YOU WILL LEARN:

- Strategies for finding your dream car

- Using the Internet for research

- Pros and cons of buying from a dealer

Stories abound about the person who answered an advertisement for a 1967 Chevrolet listed for $500 and found an original 1967 Corvette under the covers. Usually, it has something to do with the seller's son who bought the car just before leaving for Vietnam, never to return. I've never known anybody who has had this happen. You may want to search in a more conventional manner.

You can find your collector car in any number of places. If you're lucky, you might answer an ad for a 1967 Chevrolet just across town. The seller is asking $500 for the car. You arrive to find a 1967 Corvette with a 427-cubic-inch engine parked under a cover in the garage. The car will have only 3,000 original miles on it, and the story will go something like this: The seller's husband purchased the car brand new in 1967 while he was going through a midlife crisis. Shortly after, he ran away with his 20-year-old secretary, never to return. The car has been sitting in the garage ever since, and as far as the seller is concerned, it is nothing more than a 40-year-old used car that can't possibly be worth more than $500.

There are many variations of this story, some happier and some

sadder. I've heard at least a hundred of them. However, I don't know anybody firsthand who has actually bought a car under these circumstances. Unless you are one of those lucky few people who lead a charmed life, you'll probably have to find a collector car using one of the more conventional means.

Now that you've decided that you're going to buy a collector car, the urge to purchase it may be overwhelming. You must overcome that urge. Remember, patience is a virtue. This saying traces back to William Langland's epic poem "Piers the Plowman" from 1377. I doubt there were many collector cars back then, but he was probably referring to his search for a collector horse. The important point is that this saying

has stood the test of time—centuries in fact—and for good reason. There is absolutely no more valuable trait in your search for a collector car than patience.

Beauty, condition, rarity, and value are all relative terms. If your search for a collector car has not encompassed a sufficient number of cars, you cannot make valid comparisons. You may fall in love with the first 1965 Mustang Convertible you see because it is beautiful and in great condition. But with what are you comparing it to? How do you know the next one won't be even more beautiful and in even better condition? There is nothing worse than buying the car of your dreams solely because you're afraid of losing it and then seeing an even better one for less money a short time later. Veterans of the collector car hobby—at least the smart ones—often say, "There will always be another one." They have

learned this lesson the hard way. Patience, patience, patience.

PUBLICATIONS

There are many publications listing collector cars for sale, and the most famous of all is undoubtedly *Hemmings Motor News*. The monthly publication is the Bible of the collector car hobby and has been

Woulda, Coulda, Shoulda

Anthony had always admired the design of the 1970 Cadillac DeVille, and he decided he wanted to buy both a coupe and a convertible of that year to add to his car collection. Anthony had very good taste and was only interested in very-low-mileage cars that were completely original, including the paint.

I met Anthony when he responded to an advertisement for a car I was selling. It was a completely original 1970 Coupe DeVille in the stunning color combination of dark blue with a white leather interior, and it had only 16,000 original miles. We struck a deal, and Anthony was the new owner of this beautiful Cadillac. He asked me if I would keep an eye open for a DeVille convertible of the same year, and of course, I agreed.

Over the next few months, Anthony called me about several DeVille convertibles he was interested in buying. I discouraged him from buying any of them for a number of reasons, including elusive sellers, inflated prices, and lack of documentation. Anthony was getting impatient and was willing to lower his standards to include cars without the original paint. I implored him to be patient, and I assured him his patience would eventually reward him.

A few months later, Anthony called me to tell me a local dealer had contacted him and had a 1970 DeVille convertible for sale. It met all of his criteria, and the dealer was asking $30,000 for it. I told Anthony this was a lot of money for a car of this type, particularly at that time. Anthony asked me if I would take a look at it anyway, to which I agreed. I made an appointment with the dealer to see the car the following morning.

On the way to see the car, I stopped for breakfast at the local diner. Over an iced coffee, I perused the collector car section of my local newspaper, as I do almost every morning. Someone was advertising a 1970 Cadillac DeVille convertible in the same colors and with the same mileage as the one I was going to see. Coincidence? I think not! This had to be the same car, but the telephone number was not the dealer's. Most importantly, the car was offered at $15,000— half the price the dealer was asking!

I called the telephone number in the advertisement and spoke with the owner of the car. I learned he was an elderly gentleman who had purchased the car when it was new. All the questions I asked him led me to believe this was, in fact, the same car. I told him I would like to see the car, and he informed me the car was presently on consignment at a dealer in the next county. Aha! This was the same car!

I politely asked him why he was advertising the car if it was on consignment at a dealer? He informed me that, after placing the advertisement, he had decided he would prefer not to deal with the general public, and letting the dealer sell it would be easier for him. He had cancelled the advertisement, but it was too late to prevent it from appearing in the newspaper for that one day.

I proceeded to the dealer to have a look at the car, and it was exactly as described—spectacular. By 10:00 a.m., I was on the phone with Anthony informing him I felt he should buy the car and explaining the unusual circumstances surrounding the price.

Anthony asked my opinion as to how and with whom to proceed, the dealer or the owner? Honesty is always the best policy, and this case was no exception. I suggested Anthony call the dealer and inform him he was aware of the seller's unintended advertised price for the car and offer to pay him that price plus a fair commission. Anthony did so, and after a bit of haggling, he purchased the car for $18,000. Included in this price, the dealer performed a complete detailing and handled all the registration paperwork. Everybody was happy.

Anthony waited for the right car at the right price from the right seller, and his patience paid off.

1,000s OF EXOTIC & COLLECTOR CARS FOR SALE

duPont REGISTRY™

NOVEMBER 2005

A BUYERS GALLERY OF FINE AUTOMOBILES®

NOVEMBER 2005
$6.95 US
$7.95 CANADA
£4.05 UK
37330

NOVITECH ROSSO
FERRARI F430 SPIDER

HENNESSEY VIPER
SRT10 VENOM AERO BODY

Uncovered... See page 48

SPECIAL Aftermarket Edition
Aero Packages, Performance Upgrades, Wheels and more

0 70989 37330 3   11>

If you have to ask how much is costs, you can't afford it. Many of the cars listed in the *DuPont Registry* are listed without prices because many of them are priced at over $1,000,000. The photography is excellent, and the cars are beautiful. That alone makes it worth the newsstand price.

Don't overlook your local newspaper as a source of collectible cars, as many newspapers have classified sections devoted to them. If you are lucky enough to find the type of car you are looking for locally, you can eliminate many of the problems associated with purchasing a collectible car at a long distance.

for many years—deservedly so. It has the largest and most diverse listing of cars and parts for sale in one publication. Additionally, it has educational and informative columns. It is a great place to shop, but not necessarily a great place to buy. *Hemmings Motor News* tends to cater to the more sophisticated seller who is trying to realize the highest possible value for his collector car.

Since there is usually a lead time of at least a month from the time an ad is placed until the time it is published, you will usually be dealing with a less motivated and more patient seller who is willing to hold onto the car a little longer to get the price he wants. That is not to say that there aren't bargains to be had, but you're more likely to pay a higher price. There are many other national publications that are more marque-specific such as *Chevrolet & Corvette Trader* and *Mustang & Ford Trader*.

Your local bookstore magazine rack contains a wealth of information. On this rack alone, there were six magazines dealing with collectible cars in general, four magazines specifically dealing with collectible Mustangs, five for Corvettes, two for Pontiacs, and many others.

If you feel you are in the big leagues, you may peruse the pages of *The Dupont Registry* or *The Robb Report*. There are also numerous local publications. Take a trip to your local bookstore, and go to the magazine rack. You will likely find many periodicals offering collector cars for sale. Order a double chocolate latte and sit down. You'll be there for a while.

Naturally, check your local newspaper. Most major newspapers nowadays have a section devoted to collector and classic cars. Maybe you'll get lucky and find the car of your dreams for sale right in your own hometown. You would be surprised how many times I've been at a show hundreds or thousands of miles from my home only to discover a car that I'm interested in is from my hometown!

CAR SHOWS AND CRUISE NIGHTS

Another excellent place to find collector cars for sale is at car shows and cruise nights. Although these events are not specifically designed to sell collector cars, there are usually many cars for sale. If you see a car you like, talk to the owner. He may not be planning to sell the car, but if you plant the idea in his head and leave him your telephone

number, you just might get a call. This method generally works best if you speak loudly and clearly and express a genuine interest within earshot of a guy's wife or lady's husband. Quite often, there will be a message on your answering machine when you get home. These venues are also good hunting grounds because they are very personal. You will be looking at a real car and talking to a real person, instead of looking at a photo and talking to someone over the telephone.

CAR CLUBS

Many people you speak with will be members of car clubs, and they can give you leads. Usually, they will be happy to talk to you at length. Remember my very early warning about talking and talking and talking? This is where you can make it pay off for you. Don't be afraid to

Car shows and cruise nights are excellent places to talk with people about the type of collector car you're considering. Make sure you search up and down every row and aisle. You never know what you'll find.

Everything's for sale for the right price, even if it doesn't have a "For Sale" sign. If you see a car you're interested in, talk to the owner. He may be considering selling. You may just be in the right place at the right time.

ask for contacts and telephone numbers. Likewise, don't be afraid to leave your telephone number. You are now in a hunt for a collector car, and if you cast a wide net, you just might catch something.

THE INTERNET

One of my favorite places to shop, but not necessarily buy, is online. The internet has more collector cars for sale than any dealer any place on earth. Buying a car online has its dangers, but you should not ignore it just for that reason. There are ways to avoid many of the pitfalls of finding and buying a car on the internet, and we'll discuss those later.

Basically, there are three different kinds of sites on which to search. The first belong to dealers and individuals and are used for the purpose of selling cars. If you were to go to a search engine and type in "Lincoln Continental convertible for sale," there would be 285,200 returns. Trust me, I just tried it. Of course, not all of these will be cars for sale, but many of these sites are from individuals selling their personal cars, and some are from dealers selling multiple cars. This is a great way to comparison-shop from the comfort of your home.

The second kind of site I call online publications. One of

the largest is Trader Online (www.traderonline.com). They have a section dedicated to collector cars that had 141,880 listings at the time of this writing. Another is *Hemmings Motor News* (www.hemmings.com). On both of these sites, you can narrow down your search by any number of criteria, including the distance from your home.

The third type of site you will want to check is the online auction site. There are several of these, but

without a doubt the largest is eBay (www.eBay.com). Buying a car via an oline auction site is fraught with the double danger of buying a car at auction as well as buying a car online. There are ways to overcome these dangers, and we'll speak about them later.

AUCTIONS

If you plan to buy at an auction, you had best be an educated buyer or bring one with you. While you're at

The internet is an excellent place to do research. It also has thousands of collector cars for sale. This is a great way to compare models, features, and prices. Note the boxes where you can fill in your search criteria. As a car collector, I often wonder how we ever got along without the internet.

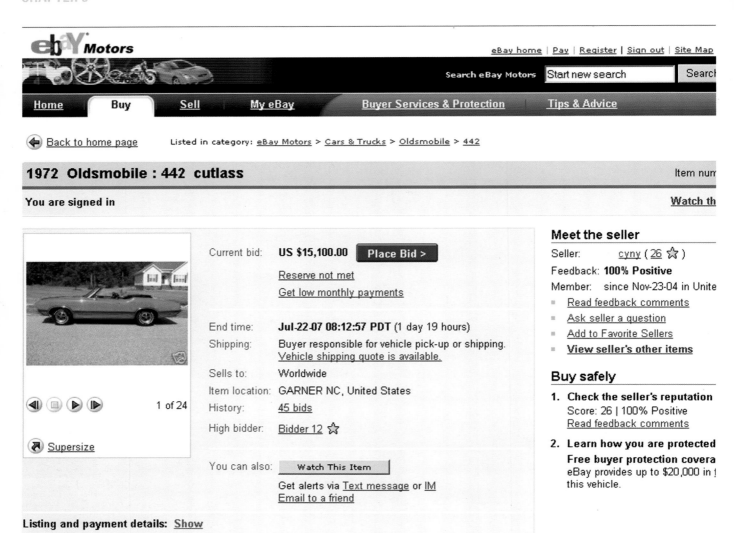

The largest internet auction site for collector cars is eBay. At any given time, there are thousands of collector car auctions taking place which can be sorted by various criteria, including the distance from your home, making it easier to locate a collector car locally. (www.ebay.com)

it, bring along a mechanic also. Caveat emptor has never been more applicable to anything in history than buying a collector car at an auction. I'll discuss this in Chapter Seven.

PRIVATE SELLER VS. DEALER

In your search for a collector car, you will likely encounter both private individuals and dealers. This naturally raises the question: from whom are you better off buying a car? There are pros and cons to both, and I mean pros and cons in both senses of the words.

There are advantages to buying a car from a dealer. Dealers often

have a wide variety of cars from which to choose. They may even be able to offer some expertise on the subject. Most diligent dealers will research the make and model of car they are trying to sell in an effort to help them sell the car. Additionally, in the event a car you purchase is substantially misrepresented, you may have some level of recourse against a dealer. A dealer is also more likely to remedy small problems with a car to close a sale. However, you must remember that dealers are in business first and foremost to make a profit. They do this by selling cars—as many cars as possible.

Live auctions are another place to search for a collector car. They can be a lot of fun to attend, but the frenzied atmosphere can cause you to make a mistake you will regret. Caveat emptor has never been more applicable to anything than collector car auctions.

In many instances, a dealer will not have extensive knowledge of a vehicle's history and may not be aware of problems with a car. Although most collector cars are sold as-is, this does not have to be the case. If a dealer agrees to correct any problems with a car, make sure to add this in writing to the sales contract.

BUYERS GUIDE

IMPORTANT: Spoken promises are difficult to enforce. Ask the dealer to put all promises in writing. Keep this form.

Ford *Mustang* *1971* *1F01M15102*
VEHICLE MAKE   MODEL   YEAR   VIN NUMBER

SN B42
DEALER STOCK NUMBER (Optional)

WARRANTIES FOR THIS VEHICLE:

☒ **AS IS - NO WARRANTY**

YOU WILL PAY ALL COSTS FOR ANY REPAIRS. The dealer assumes no responsibility for any repairs regardless of any oral statements about the vehicle.

☐ **WARRANTY**

☐ FULL   ☐ LIMITED WARRANTY. The dealer will pay _____ % of the labor and _____ % of the parts for the covered systems that fail during the warranty period. Ask the dealer for a copy of the warranty document for a full explanation of warranty coverage, exclusions, and the dealer's repair obligations. Under state law, "implied warranties" may give you even more rights.

SYSTEMS COVERED: DURATION:

Sold as is

☐ SERVICE CONTRACT. A service contract is available at an extra charge on this vehicle. Ask for details as to coverage, deductible, price, and exclusions. If you buy a service contract within 90 days of the time of sale, state law "implied warranties" may give you additional rights.

PRE PURCHASE INSPECTION: ASK THE DEALER IF YOU MAY HAVE THIS VEHICLE INSPECTED BY YOUR MECHANIC EITHER ON OR OFF THE LOT.

SEE THE BACK OF THIS FORM for important additional information, including a list of some major defects that may occur in used motor vehicles.

REORDER FROM: **LOWE'S INC.** - 2160 Harry Byrd Hwy., Darlington, S.C. 29532 - (843) 393-6127 - 1-800-845-6052 - FAX (843) 395-0468

Dealers often have wide varieties of cars to choose from, such as this Tucker. Talk to people who know the dealer to check his reputation. Contact the Better Business Bureau and the local chamber of commerce in the town where the dealer operates. News travels fast about a dishonest dealer.

This leads to the one big disadvantage of buying a car from a dealer. In many, if not most instances, dealers will not know any extensive history about a particular car. They may have an extensive photo album or paper trail, but this is not the same as having owned the car for a long time. In fact, a dealer often doesn't even own the car he's selling. Many dealers take cars on consignment, and you are actually buying the car from the individual owner. The dealer is simply acting

as a representative. When the dealer presents you the sales contract, you will discover the dealer is absolving himself of all liability that may arise. Rarely are there any warranties on a collector car. When buying a car from a dealer, get as much information in writing as possible, and be as specific as possible. When you buy a car from a dealer, what you see is what you get!

I emphasize that many dealers are as honest as they can be, given

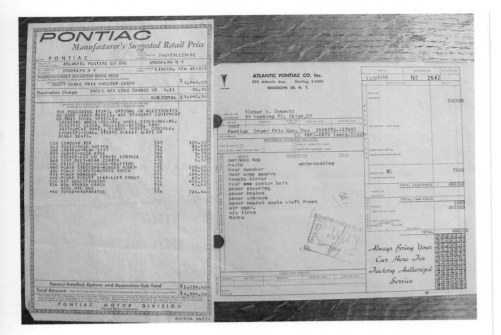

Finding a car being sold by the original owner is like finding the Holy Grail. Most people don't keep a car for 30, 40, or 50 years. Few cars last that long. You will be even luckier if the seller has retained documents like the original window sticker and bill of sale.

PONTIAC
Manufacturer's Suggested Retail Price

MAKE	PONTIAC	VEHICLE IDENTIFICATION NUMBER	266577E127692
DEALER TO WHOM DELIVERED	ATLANTIC PONTIAC CO INC		BROOKLYN N Y
DELIVERED TO DEALER AT	BROOKLYN N Y	FINAL ASSEMBLY POINT	LINDEN, NEW JERSEY

MANUFACTURER'S SUGGESTED RETAIL PRICE:
(Includes Federal Excise Tax and Suggested Dealer Delivery and Handling Charge)

SERIES & MODEL 26657 GRAND PRIX HARDTOP COUPE		$3,549.00
Destination Charge:	INCLS AIR COND CHARGE OF 4.11	96.36
	SUB-TOTAL	$3,645.36

MANUFACTURER'S SUGGESTED RETAIL DELIVERED PRICES ON OPTIONS AND ACCESSORIES INSTALLED ON THIS VEHICLE BY THE MANUFACTURER

THE FOLLOWING ITEMS, OPTIONS OR ACCESSORIES ON SOME OTHER MODELS, ARE STANDARD EQUIPMENT ON THIS MODEL VEHICLE. STEERING WHEEL-DELUXE, WHEEL DISCS-DELUXE, ELECTRIC CLOCK, MOULDING-DECOR, PAD-INSTRUMENT PANEL, FENDER SKIRTS, CONSOLE, EXHAUSTS-DUAL, STRATO BUCKET SEATS OR BENCH SEATS.

C08	CORDOVA TOP	SVT	105.32
U63	RADIO-PUSH BUTTON	342	86.89
U80	SPEAKER-REAR SEAT	351	15.80
B93	GUARDS-DOOR EDGE	382	4.74
D33	MIRROR-O/S LH REMOTE CONTROL	394	7.37
A68	SEAT BELT-REAR CENTER	432	6.32
900	PAINT STRIPE-SIDE-DELETION	491	
N40	POWER STEERING-WONDER TOUCH	501	105.25
J50	POWER BRAKES-WONDER TOUCH	502	42.10
A31	POWER WINDOWS	551	104.00
A46	POWER BUCKET SEAT-LEFT FRONT	564	69.51
C60	AIR CONDITIONING	582	421.28
P26	WSW 855X14 RAYON	TE8	43.66
	4BBL HYD ENG	XJ	
M40	TURBO-HYDRAMATIC	77M	226.44

Factory Installed Options and Accessories-Sub-Total	$1,238.68
Total Amount: (Does not include dealer installed options or accessories, state or local taxes or license fees)	$4,884.04

This label and the information thereon has been affixed to this motor vehicle by Pontiac Motor Division, General Motors Corporation, pursuant to the requirements of Public Law 85-506, 85th Congress, which prohibits the removal or alteration of this label prior to the time that such automobile is delivered to the actual custody and possession of the ultimate purchaser.

PONTIAC MOTOR DIVISION
General Motors Corporation

02-036 14229

Once you've purchased your collector car, you can accessorize your garage. Old gasoline signs, gas pumps, and air pumps make great conversation pieces.

Keeping Notes

You've identified several collector cars in which you're interested. What do you do now?

Do your homework! I'm not kidding. Get out your notebook with the black marbled cardboard cover, and make a section for each one of the cars. You will be gathering information on each car, and if you think you will be able to remember all the details of each respective car, you're wrong. Try this test. Remember our restored red Lincoln Continental convertible in Arizona. Can you tell me all of the work done during the restoration? I didn't think so, and that was just a few pages back, and the list wasn't even that long.

the limited information they may have about a particular car. After all, they do have an incentive to make you happy. Hopefully you'll tell all of your friends how fairly the dealer treated you, and maybe you'll even buy your next collector car there. Many dealers work very hard to acquire excellent examples of collector cars, but unfortunately, some do not.

Buying a car from an individual owner also has advantages and disadvantages. The big advantage is the chance that this person has owned the car for a long time, and you should be able to learn about the car's history in great detail during the time of this ownership. It's even better if the present owner, as well as previous owners, kept detailed maintenance records. You may even be lucky enough to find a collector car being sold by the original owner. Think about this: This person actually walked into a showroom 30, 40, or even 50 years ago and purchased this car when it was new. Often, they will have retained the original window sticker or bill of sale. These ordinary documents have now taken on historical significance.

The same caveats that apply to dealers also apply to individual owners. A short ownership history negates the advantages of buying a collector car from an individual rather than a dealer. And, just like dealers, some sellers are honest, and some are not. Additionally, if the seller misrepresents the car, you will have little, if any, recourse.

Chapter 6

NEGOTIATE THE DEAL

During your initial telephone call, try to determine whether the car has any characteristics that might eliminate it as a candidate. For example, if you're not sure what this piece of steel sticking up through the floor is, you will probably want a car equipped with an automatic transmission.

Find out if the seller has legal ownership of the car and has the legal documents to transfer ownership. People generally do not look at these documents very often, and when they try to find them, they can't. If the vehicle has not been registered in a long time or has never been registered in the seller's name, this problem can be difficult to overcome.

MAKE THE CALL

Once you've located a car that interests you, the first thing to do is telephone the owner and ask some basic questions about the car. You are trying to find out if the car has any characteristics that would eliminate your interest. For

example, you may only be interested in purchasing a car with an automatic transmission, and this car may have a four-speed.

During this phone call, you will ask if the owner has legal ownership of the car and the necessary documents to transfer ownership. Assuming the seller has these documents, ask to see them when you come to look at the car. If the seller is not legally able to transfer ownership, there is no point wasting time, no matter how nice the car is. There are some instances, such as estate sales, when a seller is awaiting documentation that will allow the transfer of ownership of the car. You may wish to proceed, but do not under any circumstances buy the car and pay for it until the seller can legally transfer ownership to you.

continued on page 86

If the seller is not legally able to transfer ownership, there is no point wasting your time. There was a recent case in which the presumed owner of a 1965 Shelby GT-350 unknowingly did not have legal ownership but tried to transfer ownership when selling the car. He ended up losing the car and most of his money. The car was valued at over $150,000.

"This is not what I had in mind." If this is your first gut instinct when seeing a car, simply tell the owner and walk away. People have an uncanny ability to convince themselves they want something when they really don't. There will always be other cars, and you'll know it when the right one comes along.

Above: "This is just what I had in mind." Hopefully, this will be your first impression when seeing a car. If it is, this is the time to exhibit a high degree of professionalism by asking to see the documentation allowing legal transfer of ownership. For some reason, these papers sometimes disappear between the initial telephone call and the time you come to see the car.

Right: Be certain to inspect convertible tops very carefully. Some defects can only be seen with the top in the open position. Others can only be seen with the top in the closed position. Still others can only be seen with the top between these two positions. On some cars, the top is hidden under a hard or soft boot. If you don't check the top, how do you know it even exists?

Ask the seller to send you as many photos as possible. Most people tend to concentrate on photos of the body. Other areas of the car are equally as important, particularly the undercarriage. Examine these photos carefully for defects.

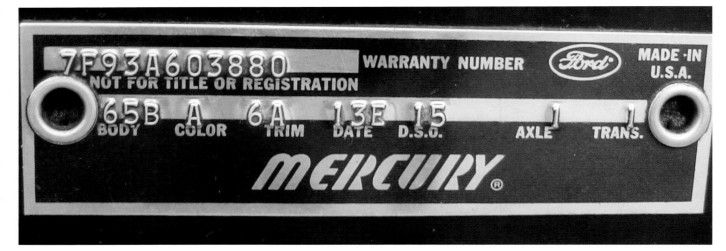

It is also important to get photos of VIN tags, data plates, fender tags, and trim tags. You can decode information from these items. This will help determine if the car is being represented accurately, and in most cases, it can be done from the comfort of your own home.

continued from page 82

PHOTOGRAPHS

Assuming the questions are answered to your satisfaction, you need to see photographs. While quality photos are important, you cannot depend on them to convey all the information you need. Remember the old saying, "A pictures is worth a thousand words"? It's not—at least, not when buying a collector car. In fact, a picture is not even worth seven words. During your conversation with the owner, he told you, "There is a ding on the door." That's seven words. Well guess what? That ding will not show up in pictures. Neither will that small scratch on the hood or the minor rust at the bottom of the fender.

So why bother with photos at all? Because at the very least they will most likely show the car actually exists. They will also show large areas of rust and dents the seller might have forgotten to mention.

If the car is a convertible, don't forget to take some photos with the top up as well as down. Get the seller to take as many photos as possible. These will include the interior, dash, headliner, trunk, and engine compartment. If you're very lucky, the seller might even know a mechanic who will put the car on a lift so he can take pictures of the underside of the car.

It is important to ask the seller to take close-up photos of any defects on the car. These would include rust and scratches in the paint, tears in the upholstery, pitting on the chrome, scratches on the glass, etc. Other important items to take photos of are VIN tags, data plates, fender tags, and trim tags.

Assure the seller you appreciate his help, honesty, and thoroughness. Hopefully, the seller will be able to e-mail these pictures to you so you will have them in a matter of minutes. At the same time, you will want the seller to e-mail to you a complete list of all documents pertaining to this car. Perhaps, the seller can photograph or scan these documents and e-mail them. This would include everything from the ownership papers to the owner's manual, as well as any receipts for repairs. I'm going to provide you with a List of Possible Documents, as well as the Personal Inspection Checklist and List of Questions.

VIN Tags, Data Plates, Fender Tags, and Trim Tags

These terms are often used interchangeably; however, each one is different and usually contains different information.

The VIN tag contains the vehicle identification number. This number may often be decoded to provide information like the vehicle's year, manufacturing plant, engine, trim, or option packages. This is not always the case though, and the information varies not only by manufacturer but by year as well.

Data plates and fender tags often include the car's VIN number and engine serial number. They may also include body styles and options.

Trim tags usually include information about the vehicle's factory color, interior colors and materials, and other similar information. Depending on the manufacturer, they may also include the date of manufacture and the plant from which the vehicle came.

Each manufacturer used their own system of tags and plates to convey this information, and these systems often changed yearly. This makes a comprehensive discussion of this subject well beyond the scope of this book. However, it is important to know these tags contain important information that may determine a car's authenticity.

You can decode some of these tags and plates with published information and the internet. Others require more expertise, and you may enlist the services of an expert specializing in a particular make and model of collector car.

Pertinent documents can be critically important. They create a provenance that will only make the car more desirable. Given two comparable vehicles, one with extensive documentation and one without, a collector will always choose the vehicle with the documentation. Often this collection of documentation may be expanded during your ownership of the vehicle through various resources.

If the vehicle manufacturer used a build sheet, this is the best single piece of documentation. Even an original window sticker can be inaccurate because dealers add options. Build sheets traveled down the assembly line and told the factory workers exactly how to equip the car. They are often hidden underneath carpeting, behind seats, and behind glove compartments.

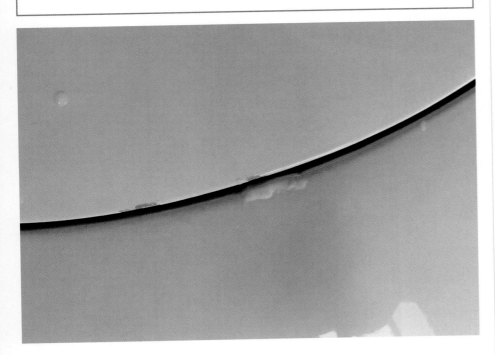

Most photos will not show defects as small as these rust bubbles. It is important to tell the seller you're interested in close-up photos of any defects. Most collector cars are not perfect. You might be willing to accept a car with a few defects, but enough small defects could require the whole car to be repainted.

This packet contains an original window sticker and an original bill of sale for a 1968 Pontiac LeMans. It was purchased at a local car show for $12. An unscrupulous person could use these documents, along with a generic photo of a matching vehicle, to create the impression they own this vehicle. An unsuspecting buyer would have no way of knowing this car doesn't exist.

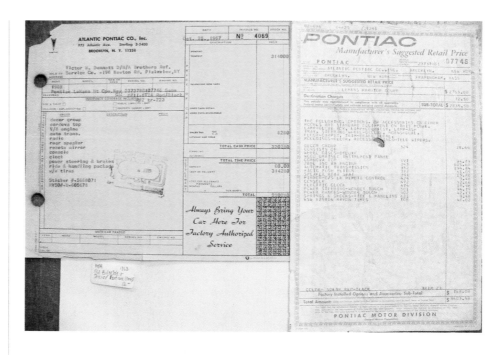

Inspectors specializing in collector cars can be found in publications like *Hemmings Motor News* or *Sports Car Market*. If you can't find an inspector in a particular area, try contacting the local chapter of a car club. For example, if the car is a Mustang, contact the Mustang Club of America.

In the event you are satisfied with the photos, you will need to see copies of several important documents before you will proceed any further. These documents will naturally include title and/or registration for transfer purposes. Depending on how the seller represents the car, they may also include items like build sheets and the original bill of sale.

Based on the photos and documents you've received thus far, you've decided you are very interested in this car and would like to proceed to the next step—the inspection.

FIRST IMPRESSIONS

If you are satisfied that you are interested in the car, and legal ownership is transferable, set up an appointment to see the car. Trust your gut instincts. If your first impression of the car is, "This is not what I had in mind," politely tell the owner and leave. Do not try to convince yourself, "This is not so bad." You don't want to end up owning a collector car that is "not so bad." Imagine how you will feel when you go to your first cruise night, and people tell you, "It's not so bad."

Let's assume your first impression is, "This is a really nice car." Ask to see documentation that will allow legal transfer of ownership. It's best to do this first

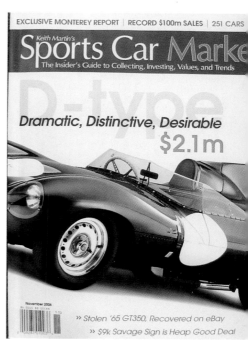

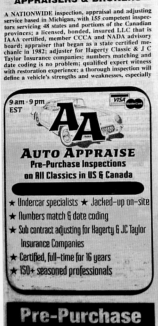

Inspectors specializing in collector cars often prepare appraisals also. In some cases, there may be more than one inspector available in the area where you need a car inspected. Speak to all of them. One may have a high level of expertise in a particular marque that you interested in. Some inspectors will give you a verbal report before formalizing their report in writing, and some won't.

for two reasons. First, these critical papers have a habit of magically disappearing between the initial telephone call and the time you come to see the car. Secondly, it will let the seller know you are interested in the car, and it will exhibit a degree of professionalism.

If you like the car, and the owner has all of the papers in order, what do you do now? Try to eliminate this car as a candidate for a possible purchase. If you are unable to eliminate it, this may be the car for you! You will now give the car a thorough inspection using the checklists found in the Appendix. If the car passes your personal inspection, you will have a mechanic or professional inspector check it out. In the event your mechanic or professional inspector gives the car a thumbs up, you may have just found your new collector car.

PROFESSIONAL INSPECTION

The inspection is where so many buyers go astray. They believe they are now in possession of enough information, that they are willing to give up large sums of money to strangers. What they don't realize is they really have very little information, and the information they do have has all been provided by, guess who? That's right, the seller.

How do we know the seller didn't buy all the documentation at a local car show and then take some pictures of a car at a show that matched the documentation? This couldn't possibly happen, could it? It could, and it does! I'm not suggesting all sellers are this dishonest, but they are biased. After all, they are trying to sell a car.

At this point, I should say most sellers I've encountered are, in fact, very honest. That's one of the great things about this hobby.

Many of today's mechanics have never adjusted a carburetor or ignition points. These items were obsolete by the time many of today's mechanics were born! The points are hidden under the distributor cap.

This engine has not one, but four carburetors!

However, even if that implies 99 percent are honest, that still leaves a lot of sellers out there of whom to be wary. Don't forget, even the honest ones may honestly be unaware of problems with their car. Classic car dealers in particular have, in most cases, not owned the cars long enough to know all the problems. Even the honest dealers who stand behind their cars can't be much help when you find out the transmission in the car that you just bought needs to be replaced.

What will you do when you call the dealer up and tell him about this transmission problem, and he kindly says, "No problem, bring it in tomorrow morning, and we'll take care of it?" As you hang up the phone smiling, you remember you bought the car 1,500 miles away and just spent $1,000 having it trucked home. Sometimes, even honesty is of no value to you.

FIND AN INSPECTOR

I cannot emphasize how important it is to have this car inspected. You wouldn't buy a house halfway across the country just because the seller said it was nice, would you?

"Where will I find an inspector specializing in collector cars?"

Many mechanics will check the tread on the tires, but they do not check closely for other defects. Tires on collector cars will often deteriorate from age long before they wear out. This deterioration often appears as cracks from UV exposure and ozone. It is not unusual to see tires that have 100 percent of their tread remaining, yet they are unsuitable for use.

Review the inspection report carefully. If there are any serious problems the seller did not disclose, it is usually best to forget about the car and look for another one. This is exactly why you had the car inspected. It is not at all unusual to have two or three cars inspected before settling on one with which you're comfortable.

STEVE LINDEN
516-524-4102 w Vehicleappraisal@aol.com

Classic & Collector Vehicle Appraisals
Inspections w Sales w Export w Consulting

Inspection Report
© Steven Linden 2000

Owners Name: XYZ Classic Auto Sales   **Prepared for:** Bob Smith
Address: 555 Main Street   **Address:**   855 West 79th Street
                       Los Angeles, Ca. 90027   New York, N.Y. 10024
                       U.S.A.   U.S.A.

Telephone: (310) 555-5678   **Telephone:** (212) 555-1234
Fax: (310) 555-7654   **Fax:**   (212) 555-6789

Date of Inspection: July 15th, 2004   **Lift Available :** Yes __X__   No _____

Vehicle Test Driven : Yes _X_ No _____   **Photos Taken :** Yes __X__ No _____

Vehicle Manufacturer: Cadillac   **Model:** Eldorado Convertible

Year: 1964   **VIN:** 64ED111111   **Plate:** ABC 123 New York

Mileage per Odometer: 77,586.9 **Engine:** 429 4 Barrel   **Transmission:** Automatic

Color Ext: Beacon Blue   **Top:** White / White Boot   **Int:** Light Blue Leather

Exterior Condition

Front Bumper: Average. No dents, dings or chrome peeling. Chrome finish is dull, but no rust or pitting. Drivers side lower bumper end rotted through at bottom. Will need to be replaced.

Grille: Average original. No cracks. Finish is dull and faded. Minor surface defects from road hazards.

Hood: Above average. Appears to have been recently refinished. No preparation defects or visible surface defects. Fit to adjacent panels very good. Underside not restored. Deteriorated hood pad.

Right Fender: Average. Appears to have been recently refinished. "Orange peel" present from chrome molding down to rocker panel molding. Extreme lower edge protruding ¼ inch from body. This is a common problem area and appears to be attributable to rust behind the fender.

Right Door(s): Average. Appears to have been recently refinished. "Orange peel" present from chrome molding down to rocker panel molding. Bottom horizontal surface of door has 1" x 1" area of rust through approximately 3" back from leading edge due to plugged drains.

Right ¼ Panel: Average. Appears to have been recently refinished. "Orange peel" present from chrome molding down to rocker panel molding. Evidence of "Patch Panel" from rear of wheel **opening to rear of vehicle indicating previous rust repair.**

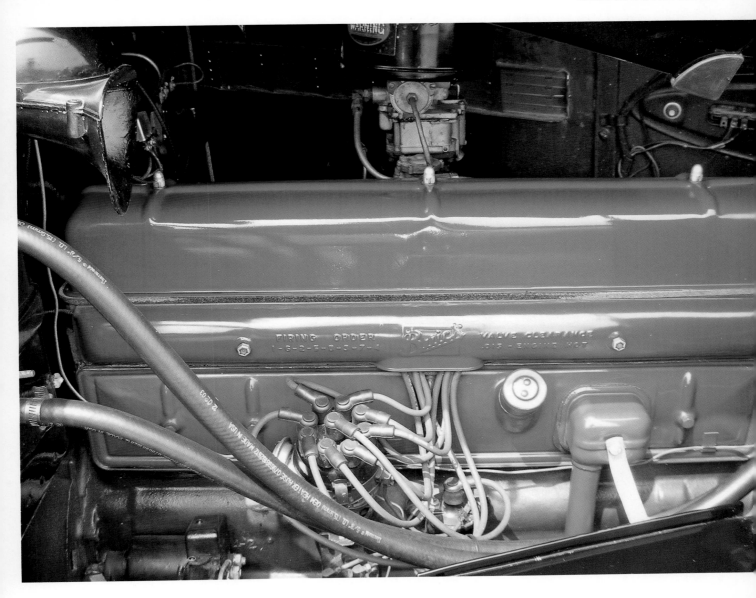

Publications like *Hemmings Motor News* or *Sports Car Market* are the first places to look. Inspectors will advertise in the classified section and will generally be grouped with appraisers. You can even do this online at their respective websites. You will find appraisers and inspectors all across the country.

There are generally two types of inspectors. Some inspectors are affiliated with one or more of the large national inspection services. They are actually subcontractors who are hired when a vehicle in their area requires an inspection. Others are independent inspectors you directly hire.

If there is more than one inspector in the area, call all of them. Find out if they have expertise in particular collector car genres. Find out exactly what they include in their reports and whether the reports will include pictures. Make sure to find out exactly how long it will take to receive the report. Often, it can take as long as 72 hours. This may be a consideration if time is of the essence.

All the time, effort, and work you've done up to this point has led to this moment. You are an educated buyer. You are pleased with the cosmetic and mechanical condition of the car, and it's now time to make an offer.

Above: **"Firm," "Negotiable," "Make me an offer." These are just some of the terms sellers use. Most sellers do not expect to sell a car for the full asking price. There is generally some room for negotiation. Since you based all of your work thus far on the seller's asking price, anything you save is money in your pocket.**

Right: **It's much easier to negotiate if you have legitimate reasons for asking for a price reduction. Try citing recent sales of similar cars, known repair costs, and transportation costs. Even if you reduce your cost only $500, that will pay for a new set of tires.**

Qualifications are another important factor. Most states do not have any certification standards for inspectors who limit themselves to collector cars. Many inspectors also perform appraisals, and most states do not certify these appraisers. Collector cars are personal property, not real property, and oversight is much less stringent. There are some private organizations that certify inspectors who meet certain minimum qualifications, but ultimately, it is up to you to determine whether an inspector will be able to do a thorough and accurate inspection.

Most qualified inspectors have a broad enough knowledge to do a thorough inspection on almost any collector car. However, some may specialize in a particular genre of collector cars. The typical cost for

Woulda, Coulda, Shoulda

I received a call from Sam, a local gentleman considering the purchase of a 1971 Plymouth Hemi 'Cuda located only a few miles from his home. He was contemplating the possibility of having the car inspected before he purchased it.

We spoke for a while, and I didn't hear from Sam for about three weeks. Sam told me the car had looked so good, he had decided an inspection was unnecessary. I knew this telephone call wouldn't have a happy ending.

Sam had a problem. He was getting a bad creaking sound from the back of the car whenever he went over a bump. He took the car to his regular mechanic, who tried replacing some of the obvious items that could cause this sound. Sam had already spent several hundred dollars in an effort to get rid of this sound, but it was still there. Sam asked me if I would take a look at the car, and I agreed.

We brought the car to his mechanic and put it up on a lift. They were very cooperative and wanted to make Sam happy. I had an idea where to look because I had seen this problem before on similar cars. I walked underneath the car and looked up at the rear frame crossmember, just above the rear axle. Sure enough, it was cracked.

The mechanic was shocked. He had never seen anything like this before. This didn't surprise me because the car was already 10 years old when the mechanic was born! How should he have known to look for this?

This was a nightmare come true for Sam. He had two options. He could weld the crack, but it may or may not hold, and even if it did, it would always be visible to any future potential purchaser. He would have to remove the fuel tank, as well as a good portion of the interior, so it would not catch fire during the welding.

Sam's other option would be to repair the car properly. This would entail replacing the cracked crossmember. This is a much more complicated job that would require a major disassembly of the rear suspension. Even this repair would most likely be visible in any future inspections, but at least it would be obvious the repair had been done correctly.

Either way, Sam was looking at a very expensive repair. Additionally, the value of Sam's car would most likely be diminished to some degree.

an inspection is between $200 and $400—maybe more if the inspector has to travel to see the car.

There is no substitute for experience, so the longer an inspector has been performing these services, the better. Experience can also apply to a specific make or model. There are inspectors that specialize in vehicles like Corvettes, Porsches, or Ferraris. In fact,

somewhere in this country is an expert in just about every make and model of collector car. Seek, and ye shall find.

If you can't find an inspector in the more traditional places, try calling brand-specific car clubs. You might even call sellers of those cars and ask them for recommendations. In the past 30 days I've had to find inspectors with specific knowl-

When an inspection is to take place, it is best to have the car on a lift. It is virtually impossible to do a thorough inspection with the car on the ground. A local repair shop will often be willing to put a car up on a lift for a small fee.

edge of Datsun 2000s, Volvo P1800s, and Citroen Traction Avants—all rather obscure cars. With a few phone calls, I found all three in short order.

Don't do anything until you receive the inspection report. This usually takes no more than 72 hours. If the inspection report indicates any serious problems with the car, forget about the car! Don't fret over the time or money that you've invested thus far. It is a mere pittance compared to what you will invest if you proceed with the purchase. If the inspection report does not indicate any problems, or only minor problems, you are ready to make the seller an offer.

INSPECTOR VS. MECHANIC

An inspector's job is to inspect cars. A mechanic's job is to diagnose and repair problems.

Collector cars are very different from the modern cars that mechanics have been trained to service. Many of today's mechanics have never adjusted a carburetor or a set of ignition points. They are not accustomed to checking for metal fatigue or dry rot on tires.

When you bring a car to a mechanic, he will usually perform a mechanical inspection. A professional inspector specializing in collector cars will generally have a multi-page checklist covering everything from mechanical condi-

Try to complete the sale at the buyer's home. Once the transaction is completed, you are the legal owner of the car. Most likely, you won't be able to drive it because you have not registered or insured it yet. The seller may still have it registered and insured but no longer owns it. If you can't complete the transaction at the buyer's home, a transportation service can deliver it.

tion to aesthetic condition. A qualified inspector will be armed with knowledge to identify problem areas. He will have obtained this knowledge by having performed hundreds of inspections.

Many mechanics do not want to perform these kinds of inspections. First, they are aware of their limitations. Second, they do not want to be in the middle of a buyer and seller. Third, the inspections are very time-consuming. The ideal situation is to arrange for an inspector to inspect the car at a shop where the car may be put up on a lift.

COMPLETE THE TRANSACTION

At this point, you should feel comfortable making an offer. You've done all of your homework, and you are now an educated buyer. You are happy with the type and model of car that you've chosen. You are also satisfied with the condition of the car, both aesthetically and mechanically. So, go ahead, the time will never be more right.

Many people approach this stage with great trepidation. They do not feel they are good negotiators. There is no reason to feel this way. You have one tremendous advantage, and you don't even realize it. The advantage is that you know the sellers' asking price, and it was the price you predicated all of your homework on.

The worst-case scenario is that you will end up paying the full price the seller is asking. If you end up paying more than the seller's asking price, you had good reason to feel you are not a good negotiator. In any case, try to negotiate. It's fun, and even if you only save $500, that represents a new set of tires for your new acquisition. Be prepared to pay for the car with a certified check or to wire money into the seller's bank account. Try to avoid paying cash if possible. It is always best to have a paper trail.

Now this is important, so listen up! If at all possible, complete the transaction, including the delivery of the car, at the buyer's location. I

Right: **Get your notebook out and take notes! You'll be asking many questions, and it will be impossible to remember all of the answers with any degree of accuracy. If you are speaking to more than one seller about more than one car, this is the only way to make certain that facts about one car don't get confused with facts about another car.**

Below: **Ask to see as many pictures as possible. Pictures are important, but you cannot depend on them to convey all of the information you need. So why bother with pictures at all? Because, at the very least, they will show the car actually exists.**

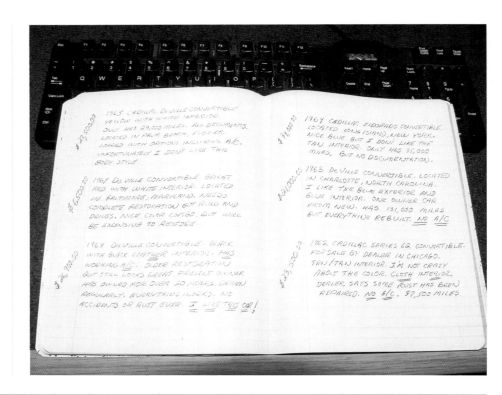

People say a picture is worth a thousand words. It's not! In the first picture, we see the right side of a 1967 Cougar. There are no major defects. In the second, we see a detailed photo of the same side of the car, just ahead of the rear wheel. That is a major defect!

can't tell you how many times I've watched somebody pay for the car of his or her dreams, and the moment the seller has been paid, he takes his license plates off of the car, and the buyer begins to wonder how to get the car home.

Occasionally, if the car is registered and insured, the seller will be willing to drive it to your home, if you drive him home. Some sellers will allow you to drive the car to your home with their license plates on the car, if you promise to return the license plates immediately. Both of these scenarios are very common, and both scenarios are fraught with danger.

If the seller is aware of minor flaws and wishes to convey these imperfections, close-up photos will sometimes capture them. Look closely at the chips just above the bumper on this 1964 Cadillac.

In both cases, once you have paid the seller and obtained the title, you are legally the owner. Most likely, you have not registered or insured the vehicle yet because you didn't own it until just now. Technically, you could be operating an unregistered, uninsured vehicle. The seller may still have it registered and insured, but the seller no longer owns it.

I emphasize the importance of completing the transaction at the buyer's home. It is the simplest way to eliminate all of these complications. If the seller is unwilling to do that, have a transportation service pick the car up and deliver it to your home!

OUT-OF-STATE PURCHASES

Buying a collector car from out of state presents its own set of challenges. The most obvious is that you can't go to look at the car in between your son's 12:00 soccer game and your daughter's 4:00 dance lesson, unless you have a private jet at your disposal.

If there is any way at all that you can go to see the car yourself, do so. Even if it is 3,000 miles away, and you don't know the difference between a radiator and a refrigerator, it is still best to see the car yourself.

Remember those gut instincts? If you go to look at the car, and your first impression is, "This is not what I had in mind," you have just saved yourself a lot of time, aggravation, and money. If your first impression is, "This is a really nice car," you can proceed with your own personal inspection, which you will follow with an inspection by a mechanic or professional inspector. Naturally, you will have addressed the ownership-transfer issues before you travel to see the car.

In the likely event you are not able to travel to see the car yourself, there are still ways to minimize your

Woulda, Coulda, Shoulda

Harry, an out-of-state buyer, contacted me to inspect a 1962 Cadillac convertible in Queens, New York. Harry told me the car was represented to him as being in showroom condition, and the seller, Bob, was asking $20,000.

For $20,000, I figured this had best be one very nice Cadillac, and I was looking forward to seeing it. Upon arrival, Bob greeted me. Bob was about five feet eight inches tall, weighed about 300 pounds, and had a big cigar sticking out of his mouth. As Bob and I walked down the driveway, the Cadillac was in view. It was also within smell. I could actually smell the fresh paint. Already, I could tell this car was at least a twenty-footer—that is, it looks good from twenty feet away, and the closer you get, the more defects become apparent. Suffice it to say, this is not a good thing.

Bob repeatedly said, "She's a beauty, ain't she?" I assured Bob, "I had seen many Cadillacs, and this was certainly one of them." He seemed pleased. Upon closer inspection, it was very easy to tell this car had undergone a rapid cosmetic restoration. I was paid to do a complete inspection, so I did, during which I found numerous significant mechanical and cosmetic problems.

As I was leaving Bob's house, he said, "So honestly, how did she do?" I told Bob, "Your Cadillac definitely compares with other Cadillacs I've seen." I'm not quite certain what that means, but Bob was happy, so I was happy. Harry had asked me to call him when I completed the inspection. He wanted my impressions before I had formalized the report. I'm never happy to give someone this kind of news, but Harry took it well.

He called me a few days later to inspect another Cadillac in Connecticut. I gave Harry a favorable report on that car, and he bought it. Several weeks later, Harry e-mailed me saying the car had just won first place in its class at a car show. Imagine what would have happened if Harry had purchased Bob's Cadillac!

risk and successfully complete a transaction. When you call the seller, let him know you are going to require a little bit of their time. Better to have to wait for a more convenient time than get abbreviated answers because the seller is in a rush. Make sure your notebook is at hand. After ascertaining the car is still available, find out about the seller's ability to transfer ownership. As we've already learned, there is no point in wasting time. This is the time to ask all your questions. I have provided you with a list of questions in the Appendix.

Chapter 7

THE AUCTION OPTION

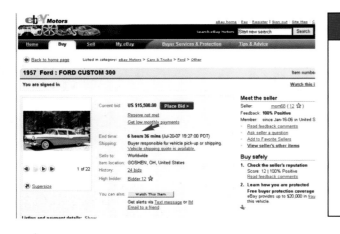

WHAT YOU WILL LEARN:

- Different types of auctions

- Pros and cons of live auctions

- Minimizing auction risks

There are inherent risks in buying any car located a long distance from your home. These risks are the same if you are considering buying a car in an online auction. However, in an online auction there is a time limit in which you must negate or minimize these risks. There are 6 1/2 hours remaining in this auction.

LIVE AUCTIONS

Imagine this: In the short span of several hours, you will search through hundreds of collector cars trying to find one that interests you. Assuming you do find one, you probably won't find its owner, so forget about asking any questions. Since you can't ask questions, you can't ask to thoroughly inspect the car. You can also forget about test-driving it.

The best you can hope for is to have your mechanic give the car a thorough visual inspection. At some point, you will probably meet the owner and hear the engine run. Unfortunately, that will be when the car's auction number is called, and it is driven up to the auction block. This is not a good time to talk to the owner. Often, you will see the owner trying to maneuver several

tons of steel through several layers of flesh and bones, while people are crowding around the moving car asking, "Do the numbers match? Is it the original paint? How does the transmission shift? Why are you selling it? Does it come with the stuffed tiger in the back seat?"

Finally, the car arrives at the auction block, and for some strange reason, several people are bidding furiously on a car they know virtually nothing about, except that it's shiny. For the privilege of buying this car, not only do they pay the auction price, they also pay a bidder's fee of $50–$500 and a buyer's premium—typically 5–15 percent. Usually, the complete process takes three minutes or less. Now, they have to figure out how to get it home. This is not the way to buy a collector car.

ONLINE AUCTIONS

Buying a car on eBay or any online auction service is not very different from buying any other car located a long distance from your home. The only real difference is, in theory, there is a time constraint. Most online auctions last between 7 and 10 days. Even if you were to find a car the day it was listed, you would have 10 days at best to complete all of the conversations, exchange pictures, see documents, and complete the inspections before the end of the auction.

This is not—I repeat, not!—a good way to buy a collector car. The best way to approach this situation is to forget this is an auction with an ending date. If you are interested in a car listed in an online auction, follow the same exact steps you would for any car located far from home. Make sure you've read Chapter Eight. If you can complete all the steps discussed in that section before the auction ends, you might be comfortable bidding on the car. If you can't complete all those steps, don't bid on the car.

The successful bidder will automatically enter a legally binding contract to purchase the car. The purchase price of a collector car may be significant enough that you may find yourself at the unwelcome end of a lawsuit, should you fail to complete the transaction for any reason. Even if you are justified in not completing the purchase, you may have to expend legal fees to defend yourself. This is not a good introduction to the collector car hobby!

In any auction, the seller may set a reserve price. The seller is not obligated to sell the car if the bidding does not reach the reserve. Naturally, the seller hopes the bidding will not only reach the reserve but surpass it. In the case of this 1968 AMX, we don't know what the seller's reserve is, but we do know the bidding has not reached the reserve.

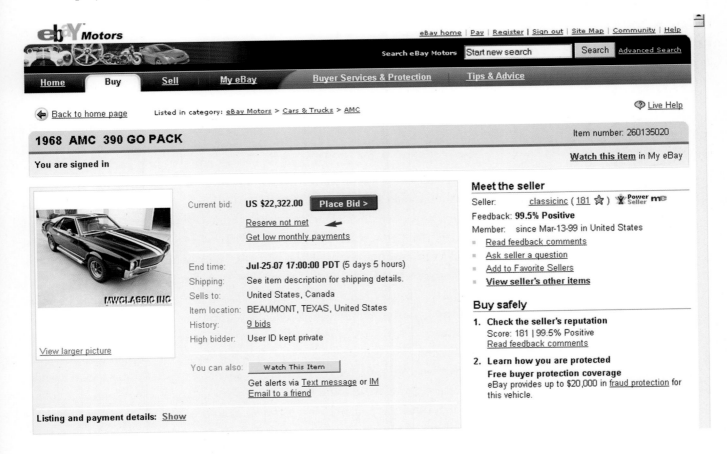

Woulda, Coulda, Shoulda

Rob was interested in buying a Pontiac Trans Am, but not just any Trans Am. It had to be a 1971 model with a 455 H.O. engine and a four-speed transmission. These are not the easiest collector cars to locate. There were only 885 built, and there is a strong demand for them among collectors.

Rob called me one day. He excitedly informed me one of these cars had just been listed on eBay. It was in Nebraska and represented as being an original, low-mileage car in very good condition. It certainly looked nice in the pictures shown on eBay. He wisely decided he was not going to try to do all of his homework in the short time the car was listed on eBay. However, he unwisely decided not to have the car inspected before he purchased it. He felt comfortable enough with the many photos the seller sent him. He even had the seller make a video recording of the car so he would be able to hear the engine run!

Rob completed the purchase and eagerly awaited its delivery. I was there when the Trans Am arrived at the shop, and it looked like a pretty nice car. Perhaps, Rob had gotten lucky. The car was immediately put on a lift to check everything underneath. We started at the front, and everything looked OK. Not perfect, but just what you would expect to find on a 30-year-old, unrestored car. So far, so good.

As we walked toward the back of the car, we noticed something very unusual. There was no back of the car. Not underneath anyway. Most of the rear of the chassis had completely rusted away. As we stood there pondering how the front could be in such good shape and the back in such bad shape, Rob arrived. His smile turned upside down when we told him the bad news.

The Trans Am had apparently been sitting with its back half in water or mud for a long period of time. This would be an expensive repair, and it had to be done. Rob spent many thousands of dollars on the repair and then sold the car. It would never bring him any enjoyment. This could have been avoided had he had an inspection.

All is not lost, however. If you do find a collector car in an online auction but cannot complete all your homework before the end of the auction, there are some things to keep in mind.

IMPORTANT AUCTION TERMS

Many sellers list their collector cars on auction sites with a "reserve." This means that, if the bidding on the car does not reach a predetermined minimum amount set by the seller, the seller does not have to sell the car. Likewise, the high bidder does not have to buy the car. You will not know what the reserve is until the bidding reaches the reserve.

For example, there is a beautiful red Lincoln Continental convertible listed on eBay. The bidding has reached $10,000. However, there is a little sign under the current high bid that says, "Reserve not met." That means the seller is not obligated to sell the car should the bidding end at $10,000. When the bidding passes $15,000, the little sign changes to "Reserve met," and the seller is obligated to sell the car to the highest bidder when the auction ends. Likewise, the highest bidder is obligated to buy the car. Therefore, we know the seller had a reserve of $15,000. Of course, the seller hopes the bidding will continue above $15,000 but is willing to sell the car at that price.

Beware of collector cars listed with no reserve. This means the seller is willing to sell the car to the highest bidder, regardless of what that bid may be. If you owned a good-quality collector car that was worth $20,000,

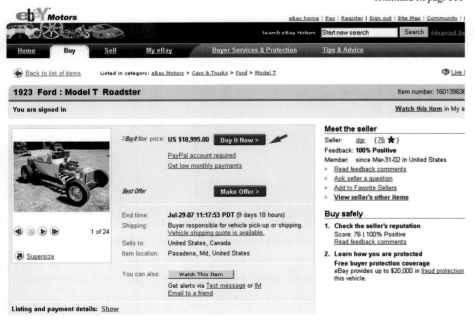

would you sell it for $5,000? That is exactly what you would have to do, if that was the highest bid.

Another option many sellers offer in these auctions is a "Buy It Now" price. That is the price at which they are willing to sell it immediately and end the auction. This price is usually at the higher end of the spectrum of the car's value. However, if you want the car really badly, and you're afraid that you

continued on page 110

Above: **A seller may choose to sell a car at no reserve. In this case, the seller must sell the car to the highest bidder regardless of how low the price may be. This is a very risky move for the seller, so beware of collector cars listed with no reserve. Some people believe listing a car with no reserve encourages active bidding, and that might be true, but it is a red flag.**

Left: **Click the Buy It Now button, and you've just bought a car. Most sellers will set the Buy It Now price at a value greater than they feel they can achieve if the auction continues to the end. You would want to exercise this option only if you desperately wanted this car, and you were afraid somebody else might choose to Buy It Now. This seller is willing to end the auction for $18,995.**

Right: **This sight will greet you when you enter one of the larger collector car auctions. There will be cars of all makes, models, and price ranges for as far as the eye can see—an overwhelming experience no matter how many times you've witnessed it.**

Below: **Although many of the owners are unavailable to answer questions, some will leave literature with details about the car. They may also leave a flier with a cell phone number. Often, they are on the premises, and they simply can't resist the temptation to do a little browsing of their own. Others simply don't want to answer questions about the car, usually for obvious reasons.**

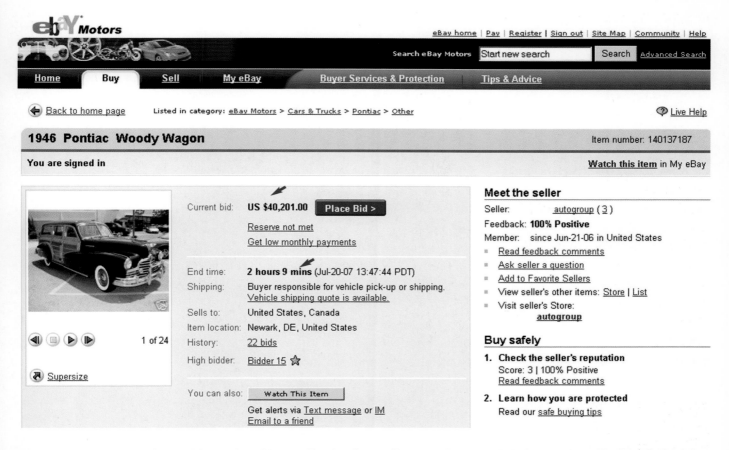

Back to home page   Listed in category: eBay Motors > Cars & Trucks > Pontiac > Other   Live Help

1946 Pontiac Woody Wagon
Item number: 140137187

You are signed in   Watch this item in My eBay

Current bid: US $40,201.00   [Place Bid >]

Reserve not met
Get low monthly payments

End time: 2 hours 9 mins (Jul-20-07 13:47:44 PDT)
Shipping: Buyer responsible for vehicle pick-up or shipping.
Vehicle shipping quote is available.
Sells to: United States, Canada
Item location: Newark, DE, United States
History: 22 bids
High bidder: Bidder 15

1 of 24
Supersize

You can also: [Watch This Item]

Get alerts via Text message or IM
Email to a friend

Meet the seller
Seller: autogroup (3)
Feedback: 100% Positive
Member: since Jun-21-06 in United States
- Read feedback comments
- Ask seller a question
- Add to Favorite Sellers
- View seller's other items: Store | List
- Visit seller's Store: **autogroup**

Buy safely
1. **Check the seller's reputation**
   Score: 3 | 100% Positive
   Read feedback comments
2. **Learn how you are protected**
   Read our safe buying tips

With just over two hours left in this auction, this 1946 Pontiac Streamliner woody wagon is below market value at $40,201. It is very common for serious bidders to wait until the last few minutes, or even seconds, before bidding. During the last two hours of this auction, spirited bidding drove the price up by over $15,000 to close at $55,276.

Arriving at an auction early is the best way to minimize your risk. This will give you the best chance to speak with the owner and inspect the car as thoroughly as possible. It will also give you the opportunity to inspect documents and break down codes if necessary. When buying a collector car at an auction, time is your best friend.

continued from page 105

If a car is popular, there will often be a frenzy of activity both on the block and off. Potential bidders will want to take one last look to see if they have missed anything. The wise bidder will maintain his composure and not place any bid that exceeds his own self-imposed limit. Keep in mind there will also be a buyer's premium if you are the successful bidder.

might lose it in the auction process, you can exercise this option.

During these types of auctions, it is common to see the price of a very desirable collector car significantly below its value right up until the last few minutes of the auction. Often, the serious bidding does not start until the last minute of the auction. Many bidders feel there is no point in bidding the price of the car up for a week or more. They would rather wait until the last seconds to place their bids.

RISKS OF AN ONLINE AUCTION

Most sellers who have a good-quality collector car are not willing to sell the car on an online auction site for less money than they would be able to sell it for by conventional means. By the same token, many buyers are not willing to pay the same price for a collector car on an online auction site for which they could buy the car by conventional means. After all, why buy something on an online auction, along with all of the inherent risks, that you could buy conventionally, eliminating most, if not all of those risks?

This leads to a very common scenario, in which the car being auctioned does not meet its reserve. In essence, the online auction has been a form of international advertising, connecting the seller with one or more interested buyers. In these cases, the transaction is often completed sometime after the online auction has ended when a potential buyer contacts the seller.

After establishing your interest in the car, you would proceed exactly as described in Chapter Eight.

MINIMIZING AUCTION RISKS

Contrary to what you may think, it is possible to buy a collector car at an auction and be satisfied, if not pleased, with the results. All you have to do is eliminate the dangers. Follow all the same steps as if you were responding to a newspaper ad or buying the car from an out-of-state seller. The only real difference is that there is a lot less time for you to accomplish this.

The first thing to do is attempt to speak with the owner. If you can't find the owner, forget about the car! Any owner wanting to sell a car at an auction has a responsibility to make himself or a representative available to answer questions. It is my belief most of the owners that make themselves unavailable do so for a reason. If they're not available, they obviously can't answer questions, and many of them prefer it that way.

Some owners do make themselves available, and a few will actually stay near their cars. Others will put a sign on the car stating they will return to the car at a certain time. Still others will leave a sign or business card with a cell phone or local telephone number at which they may be reached.

If you are able to contact the owner, find out as much information as you can about the car. Ask for any documentation that they may have. Try to find out about previous owners that you may be able to contact. Find out who restored the car (assuming that it's restored). If it is a well-known person or company with a good reputation, try to contact them.

Listen to the car run. Have your mechanic inspect the car as

An unsold car represents a loss of a commission for the auction company. To this end, they will often try to complete a sale even after an unsold car has left the auction block. If one or more parties are flexible, the sale can be completed. A seller can lower his reserve, a buyer can raise his bid, or the auction company can reduce their commission.

thoroughly as possible. Under some circumstances you may even be able to take the car for a test ride. If you are attending a multi-day auction, the cars may sometimes be removed when the day's events have ended. This is assuming that you have arrived the day before the car is scheduled to cross the auction block. Remember that you are trying to reduce your risk as much as possible while increasing your comfort level if you should decide to bid on this car.

INFORMATION IS EVERYTHING!

Assuming you are able to accomplish all the usual information-gathering tasks in the short time allotted, the results of your inquiries are satisfactory, and you feel that you absolutely have to have this particular car, then bid on it. Remember, no matter how much information you have gathered about this car, you have not been able to inspect it as thoroughly as you would have had it been for sale in a more conventional manner. Also, amidst all of the excitement,

The most famous auction is the Barrett-Jackson Classic Car Auction held every January in Scottsdale, Arizona. Many of the finest cars of their type are brought together and offered for sale. People from all over the world gather to see new price records set. Some people believe this auction determines the market for the upcoming year. Others believe it is a market unto itself.

Woulda, Coulda, Shoulda

Flying down to the auction was a given
For the weekend they'd really be livin'
After buying a car
They didn't get far
When they found out it couldn't be driven

Many years ago, Steve and Peter decided to fly from New York to Charleston, South Carolina, to attend a muscle car auction. They planned on purchasing a car together and bringing it back to New York. If all went well, they would resell it and make a fair profit. Their budget was $5,000, so obviously, many years ago actually means many decades ago.

Upon arrival, they discovered a beautiful, orange 1969 Pontiac GTO. They checked this car out to the best of their ability and decided they would bid on it. Five thousand dollars was a fair price for this car at the time. However, a 1969 Ford Mustang Mach 1 with a 428 Cobra Jet engine rolled onto the auction block first. Best of all, it was red. They had seen the car before the auction began, but had not paid it much attention. This was a very desirable car, and they felt certain this car would sell for twice, maybe even three times, what they had budgeted.

The bidding on the Mustang started at $5,000 and had stalled at $5,250. Steve and Peter looked at each other and decided fate was smiling on them. This was slightly over their budget, but how could they pass up an opportunity like this? In less than one second, they decided that, if they cashed in their return flight tickets, they could buy the car, drive it back to New York, and not go over budget. So, up went their bidders paddle and down came the gavel. Everything went exactly as planned.

Well, not exactly. Immediately after buying the car, they went to the auction office to settle their account. The sooner they hit the road, the sooner they would be home. In the office, they were lucky enough to meet the seller. He, too, wanted to leave, and he was there to collect his money. He asked Steve and Peter how they were going to get the car home, and they told him they were going to drive it back to New York. He had a puzzled look on his face, and after looking down at the ground for a few seconds, he asked them if they were aware the heat didn't work in the car. Steve and Peter weren't happy to hear this. It was going to be a long, cold drive all the way to New York. Maybe this car wasn't such a great deal after all.

When the seller realized this was not going to dissuade them from attempting the trip, he took pity on them and asked them if they had looked at the car before they had bid on it, as had everybody else. Fate was about to look down upon Steve and Peter again, only this time fate wasn't smiling. They learned the lack of heat was the least of their problems, right after lack of brakes, steering, lights, and exhaust. Fortunately, they had not yet cashed in their airline tickets. They made arrangements to have the car transported back to New York at great expense and then flew back home.

Two years and many thousands of dollars later, the car was finally in good enough condition to sell, which they did. Needless to say, they had broken every rule in the book, and they had paid for it.

try to remember you are at an auction, and you came here to get a good deal. If you can't buy this car at a discount, don't buy it. There will always be another car just like it. In fact, you may still be able to buy this car.

OFF-THE-BLOCK AUCTION SALES

The fact is, many cars don't sell when they are on the auction block. Either nobody bids on them (Do they know something that you don't?), or they fail to meet the seller's reserve. In either case, the unsold cars are usually driven from the auction block into a holding area. Here you will usually find the owner, and you can talk further.

Be forewarned, however. If you decide to buy the car from the owner within a certain time period—usually 30 days—this is called an off-the-block sale. You are still responsible to pay the auction company their buyer's premium. The auction companies will usually take possession of the title or registration papers when the seller consigns the car to the auction. They will usually not return them to the seller until 30 days after the auction ends, effectively preventing transfer of ownership for that time period.

There are a few very-well-known auctions where these concerns may not apply. The best known is the Barrett-Jackson Classic Car Auction (www.barrett-jackson.com) held every January in Scottsdale, Arizona.

In theory, these auctions attract the highest-quality cars in the country. Celebrities have owned many of the cars, the finest and best known restorers in the country have restored many of the cars. Others have come from famous car collections and have pedigrees going back decades. These auctions attract the serious bidders because they know the caliber of collector cars present will be very high, and most will be sold at "no reserve." The statistics on the Barrett-Jackson auction are staggering. The event is held over six days. The 2007 auction had 250,000 attendees. They sold all 1,240 cars crossing the auction block for a total of over $100 million.

Chapter 8

LONG-DISTANCE LOGISTICS AND OUT-OF-STATE PURCHASES

WHAT YOU WILL LEARN:

- How to pay for your car

- How to get your car home

- How to register your car

Unless the car that you're purchasing is local, you will eventually have to take a leap of faith.

Congratulations! You've reached an agreement with the seller to purchase the car of your dreams. Now, how do you complete the transaction? How do you pay the seller, and how do you get your Lincoln, while protecting both parties? This is a very difficult question to answer because there is absolutely no way to completely protect both parties during the entire course of the transaction. Ultimately, one of the parties—usually the buyer—has to take a leap of faith to some degree. That is why it was so important to do all of your homework in advance. It will give you some comfort in a situation bound to have some discomfort. This is a two-part question with a two-part answer.

METHODS OF PAYMENT

There are several ways to proceed based on two assumptions.

The first assumption is that the seller will release the car to a trucking company without being paid in full. There are some trusting souls who will do this if they have received a deposit on the car, with the understanding the deal will be paid in full immediately upon your acceptance of the car at the delivery point. This is very risky for the seller for many reasons, and most will understandably not agree to this.

Another option is for the buyer to deposit funds with an escrow service, with the understanding the funds will be released to the seller upon your acceptance of the vehicle. This is less risky for the seller because, at least, he knows the funds are there, but how does he know you will accept the vehicle? Escrow services may be found in *Hemmings Motor News*, or you can speak to your local banker. Most sellers will not relinquish ownership of a car until it's paid in full.

LIMIT YOUR EXPOSURE

This brings us to our second assumption—let's calls it reality—that the seller is not willing to release his car until he has been paid in full. This is where you make that leap of faith. You will have to pay for the car before your transporter picks it up. The simplest way to do this is either to send a certified check to the seller or wire money into his bank account. The wire transfer is the preferred method because the check can't get lost in the mail, and your bank will have a record of the transaction.

In certain very rare instances, the bank may even be able to

reverse the transfer of funds. It is important to have a clear understanding that, as soon as the seller receives the funds, he will overnight mail all the documents necessary to transfer ownership of the vehicle. You do not want the seller to have your money, the car, and the ownership papers any longer than absolutely necessary

Most sellers will not relinquish possession of the vehicle or its documents until the car has been paid for in full.

You do not want the seller to have possession of both the car and the money any longer than is absolutely necessary.

Collector cars were not always collector cars. They were built to endure the rigors of daily use, such as heat, cold, rain, and snow. Many people gasp at the thought of driving their newly purchased collector car a long distance home. This is a great way to begin your chapter in this car's history, and it will always make a great story.

because, conceivably, he could still sell the car to another party. Also, you don't want the transport company to have both the car and ownership papers for the same reason. In addition, with the ownership papers in your possession, you can begin the process of titling and registering the car and obtain insurance.

One simple way to eliminate the risk of the seller having both the documents and your money is to contact an attorney in the seller's town. You can wire the funds into an attorney's escrow account. The seller will then deliver all of the documents to the attorney, and the attorney will release the funds to the seller. The attorney will send you the documents via an overnight service. Most attorneys will provide this service for a fee of $150–250. This is a small price to pay to ensure you will receive all of the necessary documents before the seller has your money.

Another option is to have the transporter pay the seller when he picks up the car. Some transporters

offer this service. You simply send the check to the transport company, and they hand it to the seller when they arrive to pick up the car. I do not like this method because it introduces a disinterested third party into the transaction.

VEHICLE TRANSPORTATION

Now that you've paid for the car, you want to get it home, and you want it there as quickly as possible. There are several ways to accomplish this. If you are the adventurous type, one of the best ways to get it is to pick the car up yourself and drive it home. By now, you've received all of the documents necessary to transfer ownership, register, and insure the car. Call your best friend, buy a couple of one-way airline tickets and drive the car home. I've done this several times, and I can't tell you how much fun it is.

In the event this is not a possibility, or you're simply not comfortable with the idea of driving it home, you will need to have the car professionally transported buy one of two types of transporters.

It's always exciting when a huge tractor-trailer arrives, and your newly purchased collector car is inside. It's kind of like opening a giant gift box. However, both the buyer and the seller had best be somewhat flexible with their schedules because these behemoths are subject to all sorts of delays as they cross the country. Most drivers will call the recipient when they are nearing their destination to make delivery arrangements.

The first type is the large international transport company, such as Horseless Carriage (www.horseless-carriage.com), Passport Transport (www.passporttransport.com), and Dependable Auto Shippers (www.dasautoshippers.com). These companies and the others listed in

Smaller local transport companies are another option for moving your collector car. The cars are sometimes transported on an open carrier, though some do have enclosed carriers. Many of these small carriers advertise in publications like *Hemmings Motor News*. We've come a long way since this photo was taken, but the idea is still the same.

VEHICLE CONDITION REPORT

Classic Auto Transportation Company, Inc.
321 Automotive Way
New York, N.Y. 11111
212- 555-1234

Vehicle Year _1972_ Make _MERC_ Color _RED_
Model _COUGAR_ Style _CONV._ No Cyl _8_
V.I.N. _2 F92H546_
License No: _CAT_ State _N.Y._ Exp _8/08_ (Taken From Vehicle)

Customer _STEVE LINDEN_
Address _621 CARREL BLVD._
City _ANYTOWN_ State _N.Y._ Zip _13628_
Telephone _____

Deliver to:
Name Bob Smith
Address 3265 Excalibur Drive
City Los Angeles State California Zip 97213
Telephone 818-555-8765

EXTERIOR	Good	Fair	Poor	None
Front Bumper	✓			
F. Splash Pan	✓			
Hood	✓			
Top	✓			
Windshield		✓		
R.F. Fender	✓			
R.F. Wheel	✓			
R.F. Tire		✓		
R.F. Door	✓			
R.F. Glass	✓			
R.R. Glass				
R.R. Door	N/A			
R.R. Fender	✓			
R.R. Wheel	✓			
R.R. Tire		✓		
Rear Bumper	✓			
R. Splash Pan	✓			
Tail Lights	✓			
Trunk Lid		✓		
Tail Gate	N/A			
P.U. Bed	N/A			
Rear Door (s)	N/A			
Rear Glass		✓		
L.R. Fender	✓			
L.R. Wheel	✓			
L.R. Tire		✓		
L.R. Door	N/A			
L.R. Glass	✓			
L.F. Glass	✓			
L.F. Door	✓			
L.F. Wheel	✓			
L.F. Tire		✓		
L.F. Fender	✓			

MECHANICAL	Good	Fair	Poor	None
Engine	✓			
Trans.	✓			
Clutch	N/A			
Brakes	✓			
Front End	✓			
Rear End	✓			
Battery	✓			
Interior	✓			
Inst. Panel	✓			
Front Seat		✓		
Rear Seat	✓			
Door Panels	✓	✓		
Mat/Carpet		✓		
Spare Wheel	✓			
Spare Tire	✓			
Jack	✓			
Lug Wrench	✓			

Will Vehicle Drive		Yes (circled)	No

Collision Damage		Yes	No (circled)

Fuel Est:	¼	½ (circled)	¾	Full

EQUIPMENT			
Air Conditioning	Yes (circled)	No	
Automatic Trans.	Yes (circled)	No	
Other Type Trans.	3	4	5
Power Steering	Yes (circled)	No	
Power Brakes	Yes (circled)	No	
Power Seats	Yes (circled)	No	
Power Door Lock	Yes	No (circled)	
Cruise Control	Yes	No (circled)	
Tilt Wheel	Yes	No (circled)	
Vinyl Top	Yes	No (circled)	
Roof	Sun	Moon	
Custom Wheels	Yes	No (circled)	
Radio	am	fm (circled)	Stereo
Cassette	Yes	No (circled)	
Custom Exterior	Yes	No (circled)	
Wheel Covers	1 2 3 4 (circled)		
Mirror	1 2 (circled) 3 4		
Keys	Ignition (circled) Door Trunk (circled)		

Was Vehicle Locked At Time Of Repossession	Yes	No

Authorities Notified	Yes	No
Mileage	31,325.0	

ADDITIONAL EQUIPMENT OR DAMAGE NOT ALREADY LISTED

1 DENT RIGHT REAR CORNER OF TRUNK LID.
CONVERTIBLE TOP SEPARATED AT WINDOW.
BOOT FOR TOP LOCATED IN TRUNK.

SIGNED _Bob Smith_ DATE _8/21/07_

Woulda, Coulda, Shoulda

Sally bought a 1976 Triumph from a retired Navy admiral in Florida, which she needed to have transported to her home in New York. She made every mistake she possibly could. She didn't look at pictures or have the car inspected before the purchase. Sally felt the seller seemed honest, and guess what.—Sally was right!

The Triumph was a wonderful car that Sally owned for many years. However, Sally owned the Triumph for two months before she ever even saw it. Sally wasn't nearly as lucky with the company that transported the car as she was with the seller. Sally found a small auto transport company based in Connecticut—a husband and wife team who made regular trips from Connecticut to Florida—and they told her they could pick up her Triumph in Florida on their next trip. They were scheduled to leave Connecticut in two days. They would drop off their load in Florida, pick up her Triumph, and be back in six days.

When seven days came and went with no sign of her car, Sally called the transport company and left a message on their answering machine. She also called the seller, only to find the car had not yet been picked up. Three days went by before she received a return telephone call. The driver explained they had left Connecticut four days late, and then his truck had broken down in Georgia. It had taken four days to complete the repairs. He assured her he would pick up her Triumph in two days. They were very sorry for any inconvenience.

It was actually five days before the Triumph was picked up and on its way. Sally was looking forward to seeing her new toy. Three days later, Sally knew that something was wrong. It doesn't take a team of professional drivers three days to drive from Florida to New York. Where was her car? Once again, Sally called the transport company, and once again, Sally got their answering machine.

This time, it was four days before she received a return telephone call, just minutes before Sally was going to call the police and report her car stolen. Sally discovered her car was actually enjoying a trip across the southern portion of the United States. The transport company had decided to visit their daughter in Texas on their way back to New York. Sally ventured the opinion that she didn't really think Texas was between Florida and New York. They told her not to worry. They were only staying in Texas long enough for their daughter to have her baby. It shouldn't be longer than two weeks before they would be on their way. They were very sorry for any inconvenience.

After two weeks Sally called again and left a message on their answering machine. This time, it was only two days before she received a return telephone call. They were leaving Texas the following morning, and by the way, it was a girl. They would be back in New York with Sally's car in three days. They were sorry for any inconvenience.

Three days came and went, and no car. After more telephone calls, Sally found they had decided to take a relative to Florida on the way back to New York. They were sorry for any inconvenience.

Sally's Triumph finally arrived in New York over two months late. Fortunately, it was in fine shape and provided Sally with many years of enjoyment.

Sally wasn't as unlucky as Gary, who had found a small company on Long Island to transport his newly purchased 1931 LaSalle to his home in Ohio. Thinking he was doing Gary a favor, the seller had removed all of the original mirrors and lights from the exterior of the car. They are very rare—spelled E-X-P-E-N-S-I-V-E—and he didn't want them to get damaged. He put them in a box and placed the box in the trunk under the rumble seat. He did not tell the transportation company about them for fear they might be stolen, so there was no note of them on the report filled out when they picked up the car. Of course, they were stolen, and Gary was out of luck, as well as out several thousands of dollars.

Left: **The transporter should thoroughly and accurately complete a condition report when he picks up the car, and the seller should review it before he signs it. It is important the seller keep a copy until the vehicle has arrived at its destination safely. This ensures the driver's condition report cannot be changed in the event of damage to your car.**

CERTIFICATE OF TITLE

SATISFACTORY PROOF OF OWNERSHIP HAVING BEEN SUBMITTED UNDER SECTION 319.23/328.03, FLORIDA STATUTES, TITLE TO THE MOTOR VEHICLE OR VESSEL DESCRIBED BELOW IS VESTED IN THE OWNER(S) NAMED HEREIN, THIS OFFICIAL CERTIFICATE OF TITLE IS ISSUED FOR SAID MOTOR VEHICLE OR VESSEL

IDENTIFICATION NUMBER	YR.	MAKE	MODEL	BODY	WT-L-BHP	VESSEL REGIS NO.	TITLE NUMBER
0F02G119	1970	FORD		2D	3500		914471.
PREV STATE	COLOR	PRIMARY BRAND	SECONDARY BRAND	NO OF BRANDS	USE		PREV ISSUE DATE
AR	YEL				PVT		
ODOMETER STATUS OR VESSEL MANUFACTURER OR OH USE				HULL MATERIAL	PROP		DATE OF ISSUE
EXEMPT							10/04/2004

REGISTERED OWNER

LAUDERHILL   FL 33311

LIEN RELEASE
INTEREST IN THE ABOVE DESCRIBED VEHICLE IS HEREBY RELEASED
BY _____

TITLE _____ DATE _____

1ST LIENHOLDER

NONE

DIVISION OF MOTOR VEHICLES   TALLAHASSEE   FLORIDA

DEPARTMENT OF HIGHWAY SAFETY AND MOTOR VEHICLES

CARL A. FORD
DIRECTOR

Control Number 682387

FRED O. DICKINSON, III
EXECUTIVE DIRECTOR

ODOMETER CERTIFICATION - Federal and state law require that you state the mileage in connection with the transfer of ownership. Failure to complete or providing a false statement may result in fines and/or imprisonment.

TRANSFER OF TITLE BY SELLER (This section must be completed at the time of sale.)

This title is warranted and certified to be free from any liens except as noted on the face of this certificate and the motor vehicle or vessel described is hereby transferred to.

Purchaser: _____   Address _____

I/We state that this ☐ 5 or ☐ 6 digit odometer now reads ☐☐☐.☐☐☐ xx (no tenths)   Selling Price $ _____ Date Sold _____
miles, date read _____ and to the best of my knowledge that it reflects the actual mileage of the vehicle described herein, unless one of the odometer statement blocks is checked.

CAUTION: DO NOT CHECK BOX IF ACTUAL MILEAGE ☐

1. I hereby certify that to the best of my knowledge the odometer reading reflects the amount of mileage in excess of its mechanical limits.
2. I hereby certify that the odometer reading is not the actual mileage. WARNING - ODOMETER DISCREPANCY.

UNDER PENALTIES OF PERJURY, I DECLARE THAT I HAVE READ THE FOREGOING DOCUMENT AND THAT THE FACTS STATED IN IT ARE TRUE.

Signature of Purchaser _____   Printed Name of Purchaser _____
Signature of Co-Purchaser _____   Printed Name of Co-Purchaser _____
Signature of Seller _____   Printed Name of Seller _____
Signature of Co-Seller (When Applicable) _____   Printed Name of Co-Seller _____
Selling Dealer's License Number: _____   Tax No. _____
Auction Name _____   License Number _____   Tax Collected $ _____

VOID IF ALTERED

HSMV 82250 (REV. 12/02)   **STATE OF FLORIDA**

Many states issue a title to all vehicles regardless of the vehicle's age. Many states don't. If you live in a state that issues a title to all vehicles, it may be problematic to register a vehicle you purchase in a state that did not title that vehicle. This is a typical title from the State of Florida for a 1970 Ford Mustang.

Hemmings Motor News specialize in transporting collector cars in an enclosed carrier. Your car is insured up to a certain amount, which you will probably not exceed. You will also be able to call the company while the car is in transit to check on its progress. These large companies are usually, but not always, more expensive than the smaller local companies.

Which brings us to the small, local company. I know that I'll get many nasty letters for writing this, but I'll write it anyway. As a general rule of thumb, the small transporters do not demonstrate the same degree of care with the cars nor keeping a schedule as do the larger carriers, and they may or may not carry insurance. The cars are sometimes transported on open carriers.

Although many of these small carriers advertise in publications like *Hemmings Motor News*, they

New York State Registration Document

MV-639TR (6/05)   **NEW YORK STATE REGISTRATION DOCUMENT**

PAS
DMR 533
1972 MERCU   TRANSFERABLE
CONV RD   2F92H5 6598
003452 G 8 EF250208 MAR 20 2006
Wt/Seats   Fuel/Cyl   MDE SDO685
                              Expires 03/19/08

LINDEN, STEVEN, M
                              22.50
          NY
                              ANNUAL. CHG
                              AMT PAID (INCL. ADD.CHG)
EF250208 VOID IF ALTERED EXCEPT FOR ADDRESS   70.00

Some states transfer ownership via the vehicle's registration. New York did not issue titles until 1973. Any car produced before 1973 received a Transferable Registration. This is true even today. A Transferable Registration would be the proper document to use to convey ownership from the Empire State.

transport almost anything that will fit on their truck. They are generally less expensive than the larger transporters, but I do not believe the savings offset the risks. I will say that there are some exceptions. If you can get a recommendation from someone who has used one, and they can save you a significant sum of money while providing the same service as the large transporters, then you may want to try them.

Whichever transporter you choose, large or small, make sure that you make the arrangements. All transport drivers will fill out a thorough and accurate condition report when picking up the car. If for any reason they don't, send them away, and find another transporter. Make sure the seller will be present when the car is picked up, and have him check the report for accuracy. The more detailed the report, the better. This is absolutely critical. If the car is damaged during transport, you do not want to be responsible. Be prepared to pay for the transportation upon delivery with a certified check.

TRANSFERRING OWNERSHIP

In general, there are three ways to transfer ownership of a motor vehicle. It can be done via title, registration, or bill of sale, or any combination. As if this isn't complicated enough, there are two more variables to throw in. The first is the year the car was manufactured, and the second is the year that the vehicle was last registered. This means that virtually an infinite number of possible combinations of titles, registrations, bills of sale, state, year of vehicle, and year the vehicle was last registered exist.

REGISTRATION PITFALLS

Often, sellers of collector cars have not registered a vehicle in their name. When you attempt to buy the car, you may discover the title is still in the name of the person from whom the seller bought it. This is not permitted in most states, unless

In the event that there is no title or registration, you may transfer ownership by using a bill of sale. However, this does not mean you will be able to register the vehicle using this bill of sale, but it's a start. Your local motor vehicle department will advise you because the laws vary from state to state.

BILL OF SALE
© Steven Linden 2000

_____
DATE

I _____ , residing at _____
NAME   ADDRESS

_____ ,
ADDRESS

have sold on this date , 1 (one)

_____   _____   _____
YEAR   MANUFACTURER   MODEL

_____ for the sum of $ _____ .
VEHICLE IDENTIFICATION NUMBER   ENTER DOLLAR AMOUNT

to _____ , residing at _____
NAME   ADDRESS

_____ .
ADDRESS

I acknowledge receipt of ☐ a deposit in the amount of $
_____
ENTER DOLLAR AMOUNT

☐ payment in full in the amount of $ _____
ENTER DOLLAR AMOUNT

I hereby expressly state that I own this vehicle free and clear of any liens or any other encumbrances other than those that may be indicated on the title and that I have the legal right and authority to transfer ownership. Vehicle is being sold "as is, where is."

Additional Notes: _____

_____

_____
SIGNATURE OF SELLER

the seller is a licensed dealer, because the state wants to collect sales tax each time the vehicle is sold. Most states collect taxes at the time of registration.

There are an endless number of possible conflicts when buying a vehicle registered and/or titled in another state. This is particularly true of collector vehicles because they were generally produced when there was less uniformity between states regarding registration and titling procedures.

If you are considering the purchase of a collector vehicle from another state, it is crucial you determine if there will be any conflicts before you complete the transaction. Always find out from the seller what documents they will provide you with to transfer ownership. Then, check with the proper agency in your state to find out if this will be satisfactory.

Woulda, Coulda, Shoulda

In a worst-case scenario, it is conceivable you could buy a collector car from another state and never be able to legally use it in your home state.

Peter lives in New York and owns a 1964 Lincoln Continental convertible he bought a year ago from Bob, who also lives in New York. Peter didn't have time to use the car, so he never registered it, and now, he wishes to sell it. Peter is in possession of the Transferable Registration, which is the proper document for this year vehicle in the State of New York, but the registration is still in Bob's name because Peter never registered the car.

George, who lives in Ohio, buys the Lincoln from Peter, who draws up a bill of sale that he sends to George along with the Transferable Registration. George takes these papers to the Ohio Bureau of Motor Vehicles to transfer ownership to himself and register the vehicle. George is told that he has several problems.

First, the Transferable Registration is from somebody named Bob, and the bill of sale is from somebody named Peter. They don't match. Second, Ohio requires a title to register any vehicle built after 1938, but this vehicle does not have a title because New York didn't start issuing titles on motor vehicles until 1973. George calls the New York Department of Motor Vehicles and feels somewhat heartened when they inform him that they have seen this situation many times before. They tell him that they will be happy to send him an official letter stating that New York was a non-title state until 1973, but it is up to Ohio to decide whether or not they will accept that letter. Even if Ohio does accept the Transferable Registration, it still does not match the name on the bill of sale.

George calls Peter and explains the problem. George will have to send the Transferable Registration back to Peter, who will then register the vehicle in New York and receive a Transferable Registration in his name, which will then match the bill of sale. Peter agrees to do this, only to discover he needs to purchase insurance to register the Lincoln in New York. He will also have to pay the sales tax on the amount of money he paid to Bob for the Lincoln.

Peter is not happy to find out, between insurance and sales tax, it will cost him several thousand dollars before he can transfer ownership to George. Having sold the vehicle to George in good faith, Peter does this and receives the Transferable Registration, which he sends to George, who goes back to the Ohio BMV with a Transferable Registration from Peter, a bill of sale from Peter, and an official letter from the New York State Department of Motor Vehicles. As luck would have it, they accept all of the documents.

Unfortunately, George still cannot transfer ownership and register his Lincoln because the Lincoln is still in New York, and the State of Ohio requires any vehicle last registered in another state to have an official physical inspection in Ohio before it may be registered. This is not a safety inspection but, rather, an inspection to verify make, body type, model, mileage, and manufacturer's serial number or vehicle identification number. These have to match on all documents.

The Lincoln is finally transported to Ohio, passes the inspection, and George is able to transfer ownership and register his car, only because both the buyer and seller were willing to go to great trouble and expense. Imagine if Peter had refused to help. After all, he had provided George with all of the proper documents—at least in New York—and he still had possession of the Lincoln, as well as George's money.

Chapter 9

INSURANCE AND APPRAISALS

WHAT YOU WILL LEARN:

- **Types of insurance**

- **Policy requirements**

- **The importance of an appraisal**

In the eyes of an insurance company, your 1970 Superbird may simply be a 35-year-old Plymouth. In the event you should suffer a total loss, they may claim your Superbird is only worth $1,000.

COLLECTOR CAR INSURANCE

There are generally three ways to insure a collector car. The three different types of insurance vary depending on the type of usage you anticipate and your anticipated yearly mileage. There are advantages and disadvantages to each method. It is important to realize regulations vary from state to state, and from insurance company to insurance company, so this is only a guideline. It is important to check before you purchase insurance. For the purpose of this discussion, we will distinguish between your daily driver and your collector car.

The first method is to insure your collector car in the same manner you would insure your daily driver—most likely with the carrier you are using for any other vehicles you may own to take advantage of multi-car discounts that might be available.

The advantage to this method is that there are neither limitations on how or where you will use the car nor any mileage limitations. The first disadvantage to this type of insurance is that it is very expensive relative to the other types of insurance. The second disadvantage is that the vehicle will not be recognized as a collector car. If it is in an accident, or stolen, you will most likely be paid the depreciated value for the collector car. This is not an ideal situation if you paid $50,000 for a restored 1970 Chevrolet Chevelle SS you wish to use on a daily basis. If something should happen to the Chevelle, your insurance company may only recognize it as a 35-year-old-car and claim it has a value of $500.

It is very important to make sure you choose an agreed-value policy when insuring your collector car. You tell the insurer the value of the car, and they either accept or decline to insure it. In the event the car becomes a total loss, the agreed value is what you will be paid.

The second method is usually referred to as a limited-use policy in which you are given or choose an annual mileage limitation on your collector vehicle. You may not exceed this mileage. This type of policy generally has three advantages. The first is that you may use the vehicle for any purpose you would use your daily driver. The second advantage is that this type of policy is generally an agreed-value type of policy. You tell the insurer the value of the car, and they either accept or decline to insure it. In the event the car becomes a total loss, the agreed value is what the insurer will pay you. The third advantage of this type of policy is that it is relatively inexpensive. The disadvantage is the mileage limitation.

The third method is to purchase an antique or classic car policy. This is the type of policy most collector car owners choose to purchase. These policies have two advantages. They are by far the least expensive policies, and they are generally agreed-value policies.

They are so inexpensive because the insurer limits their exposure to loss in several key ways. These usually include, but are not limited to, the following typical restrictions. You may not use the collector car as a replacement for your daily driver for any reason whatsoever. Not even for a day. Not even for five minutes. For example, you may not use your collector car to commute to work while your daily driver is in the shop for repairs. However, if you have entered your collector car in a car show and you stop for dinner on the way home, this is considered a permissible use.

Additionally, the insurer will typically require there be at least one registered daily driver per licensed driver in the household. By doing this, they ensure the collector car will not be used as a

Woulda, Coulda, Shoulda

Lee called me to prepare an appraisal on his 1969 Camaro. I didn't know the details, but I knew it had been involved in an accident. His insurance company did not want to pay him, claiming he had violated the provision requiring the car to be garaged.

I was totally unprepared for the sight that greeted me. The car was crushed down to the ground, right across the middle, from the driver's side to the passenger's side. It looked as if a jumbo jet had landed on the car.

"What happened, Lee?"

He explained he was having construction done on his garage, so he needed to park the car outside for a few days. He lived in a safe neighborhood, so he wasn't concerned about the car being stolen. He had even checked the weather reports because he didn't want to leave the car outside in the rain. Dry, fair weather was predicted for at least a week. He even put a cover on it.

Even though the weather was predicted to be clear, it was also predicted to be very windy, but Lee wasn't aware of this. On the first night Lee's car was parked outside, strong winds uprooted a large tree on his property that crashed down. Fortunately, it didn't hit his car. Unfortunately, it hit his neighbor's brick chimney which, even more unfortunately, caused the entire top ten feet of the chimney to come crashing down on Lee's Camaro in one large piece. What was left of Lee's car was unsalvageable.

Lee immediately contacted his insurance company. Naturally, they wanted to know how this could have happened if the car had been garaged as his policy required. Lee explained the construction that was taking place on his garage and, therefore, the need to leave the car outdoors. His insurance company's representative thanked him for the information and politely informed him he would receive a letter in a few days denying his claim. He had violated the terms of his policy that required the car

be garaged, and they would not pay him for his loss. They suggested that perhaps his neighbor's insurance company might pay, since it was their chimney that fell on his car.

Lee was about to get an unwanted lesson in the nuances of the insurance business. As suggested, he filed a claim with his neighbor's insurance company. They informed him that, under ordinary circumstances, they would pay for the damages if their client's chimney fell on his car, but in this case, they wouldn't because it was Lee's own tree that had crashed into their client's chimney. They suggested Lee contact the company that carried his homeowner's insurance instead of his automotive insurance company. Maybe they would pay.

Once again, Lee did as suggested. He contacted this company. They informed Lee that, under ordinary circumstances, they would cover the cost of the damages if his tree fell onto his neighbor's chimney which, in turn, fell onto his car. But in this case, they wouldn't because the tree fell as a direct result of high winds, and this was considered an act of God.

Lee had unintentionally violated the terms of his collector car insurance policy, and the unthinkable had happened. Actually, it's not quite as unthinkable as you may think. I've seen many cases where a policy holder is unable to resist the temptation to drive his collector car to work on a beautiful, sunny spring day. He is involved in a traffic accident, and his claim is denied because he used it as a replacement for a daily driver.

The insurance companies are able to keep the annual premiums very affordable by limiting the use of your collector car, thus, limiting their exposure. Most owners of collector cars are able to abide by these terms with no hardship. If you feel an insurance company's policy terms are too restrictive, shop around and find one that suits your needs.

daily driver. Driving records may also be subject to scrutiny and certain criteria. The insurer will also want to make sure the vehicle is garaged properly. Curiously, there are often no mileage limitations. The insurance companies feel their exposure to loss is sufficiently limited with these and other restrictions.

Antique and classic car policies are available from companies like J.C. Taylor Antique Automobile Insurance (www.jctaylor.com), Hagerty Collector Car and Boat Insurance (www.hagerty.com), Condon & Skelly (www.condonskelly.com), American Collector Insurance (www.americancollectorsins.com), and others. Additionally, some of the conventional automobile insurers like State Farm offer policies specifically covering collector cars.

APPRAISALS

Although it's not absolutely necessary, it's always a good idea to have your collector car appraised before shopping for insurance. If you choose to insure your collector car via a conventional insurance company, such as the one that insures your daily driver, you will most likely not be declaring the value the insurance company will pay you in the event of a total loss.

Should you suffer this loss, you are at the mercy of the insurance company as to how much money they'll pay you. If you are not happy—and you won't be—with the settlement they offer, your only recourse may be the court system. This can be time-consuming and expensive, whereas, the insurance companies have attorneys who deal with these matters daily. If you obtain an appraisal before you suffer the loss, you will have an unbiased opinion of the vehicle's value. This is often a great help when negotiating a settlement with the insurance company.

If you choose to purchase your insurance policy through a classic car insurance company, you will be declaring a value you will be paid in the event of a loss. An appraisal will help to substantiate the value that you declare on the vehicle.

In any event, keep clear pictures of the car from all four sides, as well as all receipts for any aftermarket equipment that may have been added. Often, this equipment is covered up to a limit.

Chapter 10

PARTS AND SERVICE

WHAT YOU WILL LEARN:

- Maintenance basics

- Finding a shop to service your car

- Locating replacement parts

The best way to find a shop that services collector cars is to speak to the owners of collector cars in your area. Contacting car clubs and attending car shows is a great way to get a recommendation for a qualified shop.

BASIC MAINTENANCE

For many people, the relative ease of maintenance and repairs is part of the lure of classic cars. Even if you have only a basic mechanical inclination, you may find it is both financially rewarding and enjoyable to perform maintenance and repairs yourself.

Generally speaking, these cars are from a time when things were simpler. Basic maintenance, tasks like fluid changes are straightforward. Even brake jobs and tune-ups are well within the mechanical abilities of someone with a service manual and the most basic of mechanical skills. You can always choose to leave the major repairs to a qualified shop if you wish.

Many collector car owners, including myself, have discovered performing our own maintenance

and repairs is the best form of therapy there is. Aside from the obvious financial benefits, you also learn about your car much more intimately. This enhances the pleasure of ownership. Not to be overlooked is the reward of successfully repairing or replacing something that was broken.

Just as with any modern car, collector cars need routine maintenance. This is not to say they require constant repairs. On the contrary, a well-maintained collector car should be at least as dependable as it was when new and sometimes more dependable because of the better-quality replacement parts available today.

There are also many upgrades available specifically designed to make collector cars not only more dependable, but

safer as well. These would include items like kits that replace the old points-style ignition system with a modern electronic ignition system. Another popular upgrade is a kit that replaces your old drum-brake assemblies with modern disc brakes. As the collector car hobby grows, these and others become available for more specific makes and models of collector cars, and if you can follow printed instructions, you can usually install them yourself.

SERVICING A COLLECTOR CAR

So what if you choose to pay someone to service your collector car? How do you find an appropriate shop? That depends on the type of collector car you have purchased. Ideally, you would like to find a shop specializing in collector cars. The best way to do this is to find out where other collector car owners are having their cars serviced. Sometimes, it will be a shop that services only collector cars, and sometimes, it will be a general repair facility

A simple repair on a collector car can take longer than on a modern car because parts may have been bolted together for decades. Disassembly may be more time-consuming, and the mechanic may have to make many telephone calls to find parts. Many mechanics are reluctant to quote a price for a repair in advance and will charge for the actual amount of time to complete the repair plus parts.

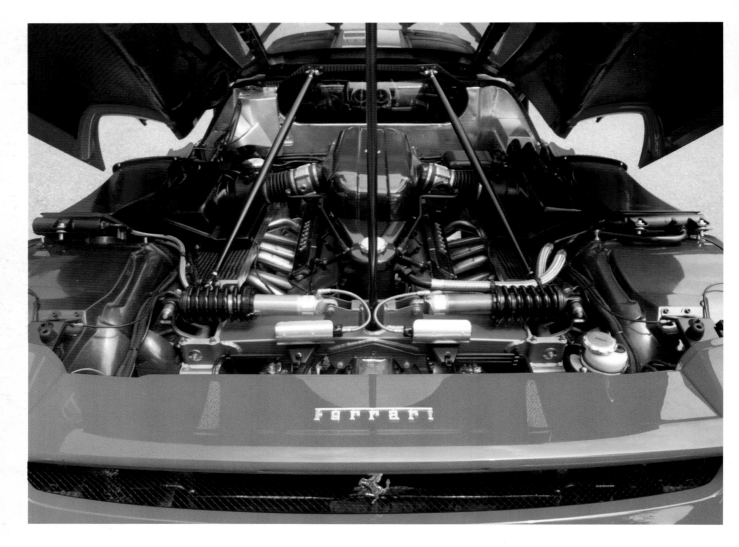

Some collector cars are so specialized they must be serviced only by specially trained technicians. Most mechanics would simply not know where to begin on this Ferrari.

known locally for quality service of collector cars. These types of shops tend to understand that the owners of collector cars have special concerns about the way their cars will be treated when left for service.

SPECIALTY SHOPS

Although different from modern cars in many respects, most collector cars are relatively simple; so any qualified mechanic should be able to service one if you can't find a shop specializing in collector cars. Some collector cars, however, are very complicated, and only a facility specializing in these types of cars should

service them. This applies predominantly to exotic foreign models. Only Ferrari experts should service Ferraris, for example. This not only ensures quality of workmanship, but it will also not compromise the car's value when it comes time to sell it.

This holds true for virtually any collector car, foreign or domestic, that has undergone a faithful restoration to original factory specifications. This might include a car like an early Corvette that has been Bloomington Gold Certified. In this case, it would be important to find a repair shop sensitive to the detail required to

maintain the car's value. The use of something as simple as an incorrect bolt or hose clamp can have a significant effect on the value of this car. It would be best to locate a repair shop specializing in older Corvettes.

By speaking to club members and searching the internet, you should be able to find a facility that can accommodate your needs.

FINDING PARTS

You might be surprised at how simple yet sophisticated the distribution network is for collector car parts. As the collector car hobby has grown, so has the parts business. No matter what kind of collector car you own, there is usually a network of parts suppliers ready and willing to fill your needs. If they can't, they will

continued on page 135

In the case of a vehicle that has undergone a faithful restoration to original factory specifications, only a shop that specializes in these types of cars should be used. Something as simple as an incorrect hose clamp may go unnoticed, but it will be a red flag to a judge or knowledgeable purchaser. This Jaguar engine has been restored properly, and anything improper will tend to stand out.

Woulda, Coulda, Shoulda

Debbie wanted to buy a classic car she could use regularly whenever her whim and the weather would allow. It had to be cute, and it had to be dependable. This would be her first classic car, so she asked my opinion about what might be a smart purchase. I asked her if there was any particular classic car that she liked, and she responded that she had always liked the clean, sporty lines of the early Mustangs. This was going to be easy, as these early Mustangs are usually my first recommendation to newcomers. They are plentiful, and there is an ample supply of parts. Additionally, they're available with engines ranging from small sixes to large V-8s. Options were virtually unlimited, including automatic transmissions as well as three- and four-speed manual transmissions. Most importantly, they are simple,

I usually recommend a newcomer buy a Mustang with the 289-cubic-inch V-8 engine, air conditioning, and their choice of an automatic or manual transmission. This provides a nice combination of power and handling, along with true year-round usability.

Debbie was lucky enough to find just such a car for sale nearby. It appeared to have been very well cared for its whole life. She was further comforted that the seller was the original owner. He informed her the car ran very well, except it idled roughly because it needed a carburetor rebuild. She bought the car, and the owner drove it to her house.

Debbie was excited, and she called me to tell me. She told me what a wonderful car it was, needing only a carburetor rebuild. I asked her if she needed a recommendation for somebody to rebuild the carburetor. I was surprised when she told me she planned to do it herself. She had already purchased a service manual and the appropriate carburetor rebuild kit. Apparently Debbie had grown up on a farm, and tinkering with things was not something she was afraid of, although, she did comment on the large number of tiny parts in the kit. Before she hung up, she said "What's the worst than can happen? If I ruin it, I'll have to pay somebody to fix it, and I would have had to pay them anyway." She asked if there were any secrets to this job, and I advised her simply to make sure that she had a clean, well-lighted place to work in and to follow the instructions one step at a time. Most importantly, I told her not to rush.

About two weeks later, Debbie called to ask me for an appraisal for her insurance company. I asked her about her carburetor, and she told me she had done it about a week before.

"So, how's it working?" I asked.

"It works fine—no problems. The car runs great," she said matter-of-factly.

Apparently Debbie was unaware that rebuilding a carburetor was the type of job many hobbyists, even mechanics, shy away from. She didn't know she was supposed to be afraid of this job, so she wasn't.

If everybody who wants to attempt their own repairs could have Debbie's "What's the worst than can happen?" attitude, the level of satisfaction that they achieve from this hobby would be greatly enhanced.

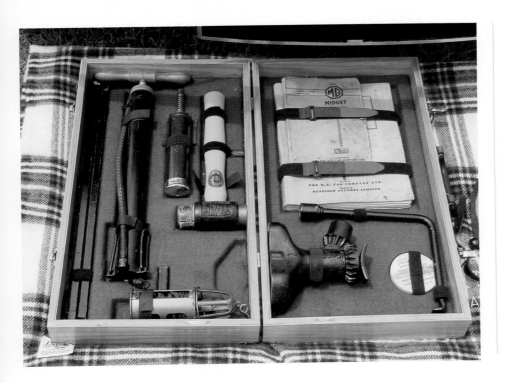

Left: These original MG tools are extremely difficult to find, particularly in their original case. Additionally, this kit contains the original owner's manual and service manual. A complete kit can be worth several thousand dollars and can add at least that much to the value of the car.

Below: One man's garbage is another man's treasure. Somewhere, somebody is probably searching for one of these parts. Many of these parts will be gone by the end of the day. If you see something you really need, buy it.

Many parts for collector cars are still available right at your local auto parts store. Tune-up kits have everything you'll need, including oil filter, fuel filter, points, rotor, condenser, distributor cap, ignition wires, and spark plugs.

continued from page 131

usually recommend somebody who can. I can't think of a single part I've ever needed for a collector car that I was not able to find in one day. Price is another subject completely. If you need a rare part, or a part that is not being reproduced, be prepared to pay an exorbitant price.

Many parts for collector cars are still available right at your local auto parts store. Common items,

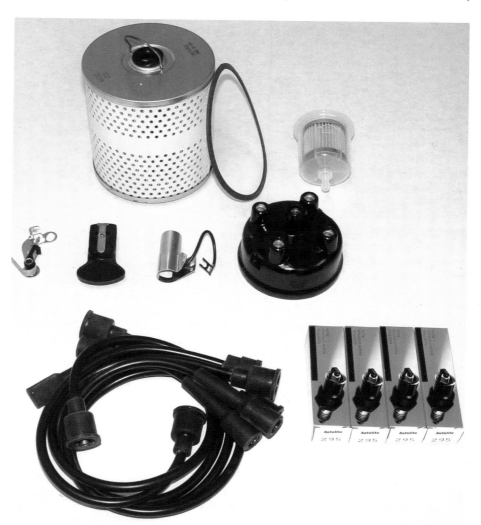

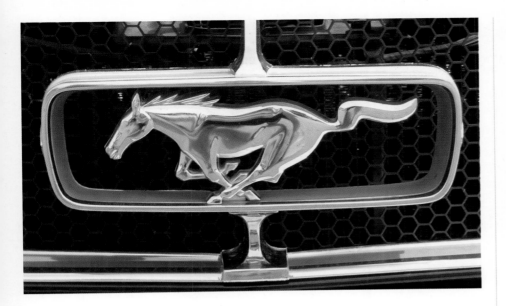

The quality of reproduction parts like this grill emblem varies, so try to purchase ones licensed by the original manufacturers. More popular models like Mustangs and Corvettes have just about every part available. New reproduction parts can be a cost-effective way to restore a car, as opposed to the labor-intensive process of restoring old parts one by one.

such as tune-up parts, starters, alternators, radiators, window cranks, and window motors should be easily available. Reproduction companies manufacture many collector car parts under licenses from car companies, and this helps keep the prices down. If your collector car has been faithfully restored to original factory specifications, you will want to order parts from vendors specializing in your particular make and model, but be prepared to pay a bit more. If the part is no longer being manufactured or reproduced, prepare to pay even more. If the part is specific to only one make or model, prepare to pay still more—sometime much more. If it is a particularly rare part, such as an original wing for a Plymouth Superbird, it might delay your child's college education by a year or two.

Hemmings Motor News is the best place to start your search, along with the internet, local car shows, and swap meets.

Chapter 11

CARE AND FEEDING

WHAT YOU WILL LEARN:

• Storage basics

• Fundamentals of car care

• Car cover considerations

Not everybody can have a garage like this. However, it is important to store your collector car in a safe, sound, dry environment, or it will deteriorate. Most home garages are perfectly adequate.

WHERE SHOULD I KEEP MY COLLECTOR CAR?

You should store your collector car in a safe, secure, dry, structurally sound garage. In fact, most collector car insurance policies require the vehicle to be parked in a sound, locked garage. You would be surprised at how many beautiful collector cars I have seen parked in wet, leaky garages that look like they will blow down in the next strong wind. Some people store their collector cars outdoors, using car covers. This is definitely not an ideal way to protect your car. Your car will deteriorate if you store it outdoors with or without a car cover. Some types of car covers actually accelerate deterioration.

If you do not have a garage, try to rent a private garage near your home. As a last resort, you may have to rent a parking spot in a public garage. If this is the case, be sure to check with your insurance company to make sure you are not violating the terms of your policy.

The ideal garage floor will have some type of moisture barrier, such as epoxy floor paint, which will prevent moisture in the floor from condensing on the bottom of the car. A fan is a good idea to keep the air circulating. Contrary to intuition, it is best to place the fan at floor-level or aim it at the floor to keep this moist air moving.

Since collector cars are often stored for relatively long periods of time, moisture can cause rust in frame rails and floor pans if it is allowed to gather. If you can see visible signs of moisture anywhere in the garage or on the car, it is best to use a dehumidifier. These units are about the same size and price as a small air conditioner and are generally portable.

BASIC CARE

Keeping your collector clean will not only enhance your pride of ownership, it will also protect your investment. If the paint is allowed to remain dirty, it will eventually deteriorate. If the interior is not kept clean and protected with a vinyl or leather protector, it will fade and crack over time. If the engine is allowed to become grimy, it may mask minor leaks that will eventually become major leaks and potentially major repairs.

I can do a major cleaning of almost any collector car in about half a day. I usually do this twice a year, and no specialized knowledge is required. There are literally hundreds of products available to aid you in keeping your collector car clean. Walk into any auto supply store, and you will find at least one aisle dedicated solely to these products. You will most likely need some form of car-wash soap, a high-quality wax, an interior cleaner and protector, a vinyl top or convertible top treatment, and an engine degreaser. Use all these products according to the manufacturers' instructions, using clean, appropriate rags and applicators.

Begin by washing the car in the shade so you will be able to dry the car before the sun does. If the sun dries the car, it can leave water spots, or even burn the paint. Use a clean sponge or soft rag and a bucket filled with a mixture of clean water and car-wash soap. Do

not use a high-pressure sprayer or even a direct stream from a garden hose as you would on a modern car, since these can easily overpower the various glass and body seals, allowing water into the car. You do not want a significant amount of water to gather in any nooks or crannys where you can't dry it thoroughly. Any place that water is allowed to remain is a potential source of rust. After you've washed and dried the car, apply the wax, according to the instructions. When you buff the wax, you'll be amazed at how nice your car looks.

If you have a vinyl roof or convertible top, apply the appropriate cleaner and protecting treatment. Always apply the product to an applicator and use the applicator to apply it to the top. If you spray or apply it directly on the top, it's likely that it will also end up on your freshly waxed paint.

The interior is simple. Just apply the products that you've purchased as instructed. One again, use a rag or applicator in order to prevent getting these products on the glass, where it will smear.

If you store your collector car outdoors, it is absolutely imperative you use the correct type of cover. The use of an incorrect cover can destroy your car's finish in one season. Outdoor covers are designed to keep your car dry, yet they are breathable so moisture will not collect under the cover. If a cover traps moisture, it will ruin your car's finish.

It is always a good idea to use a car cover, even if you store your collector car indoors. For indoor use, I prefer light-cotton car covers. This is usually the only type of cover you will be able to fit in a washing machine. Note all of the hazards hanging on the wall around this car. Each one is a potential disaster.

When using engine degreaser, disconnect the battery. Clean everything in sight, including wires. As you remove the layers of dirt from these wires, you'll be amazed at the myriad of brightly color-coded wires that may become visible for the first time in decades. If the engine is extremely greasy, you may have to soak the entire engine in degreaser and rinse it off with water. If this is the case, make sure to cover electrical components like the alternator and distributor.

If you're the type of person that would rather be out driving your car rather than cleaning it, you can usually have a comprehensive detailing job done for $150–$250.

CAR COVERS

Using a car cover is generally a good idea, even if you store your collector car indoors. Car covers will protect your car from dirt and dust. A cover may also minimize physical damage if something falls.

There are many different types of car covers available, including indoor and outdoor versions. There are universal-fit covers, and there are custom-fit car covers. They range in quality from vinyl or plastic to flannel-lined cotton. They also range in price from about $19 to well over $400. The more expensive covers are not necessarily the best for you. The way you intend to use the car cover will determine which one is appropriate for you.

Be certain to buy your car cover from a reputable manufacturer. They will ask you some questions about your intended use of the cover, and they will recommend the appropriate product. Take their advice. If you do not intend to use the proper cover, you are better off not using any cover at all. Misuse of a car cover can ruin the finish very quickly, particularly outdoors. Collector car covers are available from companies like the California Car Cover Company (www.calcarcover.com), Covercraft (www.covercraft.com), Wolf Automotive (www.wolfautomotive.com), and others.

When Not to Use a Car Cover

You should never, ever use a car cover when you are towing your collector car, unless it is in an enclosed trailer. This is a mistake I see all too often. The wind will cause the cover to flap repeatedly against the paint, effectively buffing the paint right off the car. More than once, I have seen a car on a trailer arrive at a car show with a cover on it. Upon removal of the car cover, the owner has been horrified to discover his paint job ruined. A car cover should be viewed as a tool to help you protect your investment. If it is used properly, it will do its job well.

Woulda, Coulda, Shoulda

Because of professional obligations, Claire had been unable to use her 1957 Thunderbird for the past two years. She was considering selling it, and she wanted to get an idea of the car's value, so she contacted me to appraise it. We made arrangements to meet at her weekend home, where she kept the car garaged. Her weekend home was actually an estate, complete with a moderately sized castle. To get to her weekend home, I had to cross a private bridge onto an island. This bridge was manned by a security guard. It was a modern-day moat.

Unfortunately, this estate also had a dungeon, and this is where she kept the car. She invited me into the castle to chat while I reviewed the paperwork associated with the car. The car had excellent provenance. A well-known country music singer had once owned it. So far, so good.

It was time to see the car. We left the castle and walked several hundred feet down a path until we reached a gravel apron that connected the path to the garage. The garage door resembled an old barn door. The garage itself was built into the side of a grassy hill, placing it completely below ground level, and as we got closer to the garage, I could see that the gravel in front of it was very damp. Hopefully, this dampness was not coming from the garage. I asked Claire when she had seen the car last, and she told me it had been about two years. She told me she had carefully parked it in the garage and covered it.

We stepped off of the path and onto the gravel directly in front of the garage. We each took hold of one door, stood back, and swung open the doors. The stench of mold and mildew overcame us immediately and we both stepped back several yards. I peered into the dark garage, but I was too far away to see any detail. I was able to see this garage was little more than a hole that had been cut into the side of the hill, reinforced with large timbers like the entrance to an old mine. There sat her 1957 Thunderbird under a tattered, rotted cover.

I wanted to yell at her, "What's wrong with you?," but I could see that she was as taken aback as I was. In fact, she looked like she was going to cry. When the worst of the smell had dissipated, we ventured forward to have a closer look. We stepped inside, and Claire switched on the overhead light

She assured me that, in the ten years she had owned this car, this garage had always been dry. Coupled with the fact she had used it every weekend until two years ago meant the car, as well as the garage, had been aired out weekly.

Moments later, it became obvious she was telling the truth. I spotted a rain gutter that had run along the back wall, and connected to another rain gutter that ran along the side wall, and then down into a drain in the floor. These rain gutters, which are typically used on the exterior of a house, had been installed inside of the garage to channel water through the garage and down into the drain. Sometime during the past two years, one end of the back-wall rain gutter had broken and fallen to the floor. Every single drop of water that should have

reached the drain went directly onto the garage floor instead, and there it remained. This had likely been going on for the entire two years since Claire had last seen the Thunderbird, and no air had circulated through the garage during this time.

We donned gloves and slowly peeled the remnants of the cover off of the car. A pitiful sight greeted us. The paint on the car was covered in muddy brown patches of surface rust. The chrome on the bumpers was peeling. The insides of the windows were so wet with condensation that we couldn't see inside of the car. We opened the doors. The convertible top had begun to rot, as had the leather seats and trim. Rust had invaded every metal surface, and mold had invaded everything else.

As bad as it was, I had seen worse cars restored to splendid condition, but not much worse. It would cost a lot of money to restore this car—certainly more than it would be worth. I reviewed some of Claire's options, and I told her to call me if I could help.

Even if I had seen this car in this garage on a beautiful, dry, sunny day, I would have advised Claire to move it to a better location. A dirt-walled, gravel-floored, timber-lined, below-ground-level garage with water running through it is simply a disaster waiting to happen.

This is not the ideal way to store a collector car. Even if you live in a dry climate like Arizona, there are still other considerations. Animals will most likely find your car makes a comfortable home, once they've pulled the stuffing out of your seats. Additionally, this doesn't even come close to fulfilling your insurance policy's requirement that you store the vehicle in a sound structure.

Appendix

CHECKLISTS

Check the odometer reading. Don't forget, many odometers on collector cars only have five digits. What appears to be a car with 26,729 miles may actually be a car with 126,729 miles. It is also relatively easy to turn back the mileage or replace the odometer on most collector cars. This is why it's important to check all of the documentation in a methodical manner.

Right: Ask the owner if the car has ever been shown or if it has won any awards. This could be an indication as to the thoroughness and accuracy of any restoration work. Awards like the Bloomington Gold are available for Corvettes. You can be certain any Corvette that has achieved a Bloomington Gold award is a high-quality car. At least, it was at the time it received the award.

QUESTIONS FOR THE SELLER

This list may look extensive, but the questions are very general, and the whole list may usually be completed in one 15-minute conversation. There is absolutely nothing wrong with telling a seller you have a list of questions. It is always polite to say it will take about 15 minutes and ask if this is a convenient time.

It is important to ask these questions before proceeding any further for several reasons. First, if you are not comfortable with any of the answers, you will not waste your time inspecting the car. Second, it will show a degree of professionalism and let the seller know you may get serious about his or her car. Third, it will give the seller an incentive to be forthcoming with accurate information, knowing you will eventually inspect the car, and the seller will lose credibility if not honest. Last, it will give you an opportunity to gauge the attitude of the seller.

If the seller makes you feel like a bother at this early stage, imagine how you will feel later on. If the seller has only owned the car for a short time and is unable to answer many of the other questions, the seller may be a dealer.

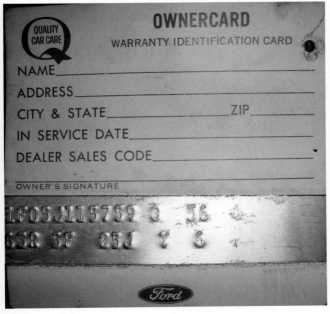

Original documents are very important in determining the authenticity of a particular vehicle. Items like original window stickers and invoices contain a wealth of information, such as the options with which a vehicle was originally equipped. This is an original factory invoice for a 1972 Cougar and an original warranty card for a 1971 Mustang. These cards were presented at the dealership when the cars were brought in for warranty repairs.

List of Questions for the Seller:

Do you own the car, or are you selling it for somebody else?

Do you have the necessary documentation to transfer ownership?

What other documentation do you have?
(See the following list)

How long have you owned the car?

What is the mileage on the car? Do you believe it to be accurate?

Can you tell me all of the accessories and options the car has?

Has the car ever been shown or won any awards?

To the best of your knowledge, has the car ever been in an accident?

What is the overall condition of the body? Can you tell me about any defects?

What is the overall condition of the interior? Can you tell me about any defects?

What is the overall mechanical condition? Can you tell me about any problems?

Is the car garaged? How often do you use it?

Who maintains the car for you?

Are you willing to have a mechanic or inspector inspect this car?

Is there anything else that you would like to tell me about this car?

Beauty is in the eye of the beholder. Something as simple as an upholstery pattern may be enough reason for you to pass on a car. Custom upholstery may have appealed to the seller of the car, but you may find it too objectionable to live with. Even some original factory upholstery would make you dizzy if you stared at it too long!

DOCUMENTATION

If you decide you are interested in this particular car, you will have to see all the documents. It is not necessary to see the originals. Copies or faxes are fine. Many sellers will simply tell you they have nothing but the papers necessary to transfer ownership. This is not an ideal situation for a collector car. Certainly, the more documentation a collector car has, the more desirable it is. This usually has a significant effect on the value of the car. There are many collectors who will pay large premiums for a heavily documented collector car. There are also many collectors will not buy a collector car if it does not have significant documentation—also called provenance.

Let's assume the seller has all the documentation listed and provides it to you. First, put all the documents in chronological order. Make a chart containing four columns with the following headings: Date, Mileage, Document, and Notes. Each document will contain all of the information. It should look something like the chart below.

What's wrong with this picture? How could the mileage have dropped by almost 100,000 miles in a period spanning just two years? This is a common scenario. Most collector cars only have five digit odometers. Therefore, they

DOCUMENTATION CHECKLIST

DATE	MILEAGE	DOCUMENT	NOTES
09/22/71		Build sheet	Found under rear seat
10/05/71		Window sticker	Copy, not original
10/07/71	00000.2	Factory-to-dealer invoice	Original
10/22/71	00000.2	Original bill of sale	
11/15/71		First registration	
11/18/71	00095.3	First state inspection receipt	
12/02/71	00555.5	Receipt for oil change	
11/05/72	09876.5	State inspection receipt	
11/16/73	21657.8	State inspection receipt	
05/16/74	32154.9	Receipt for tires	
11/29/75	38753.7	State inspection	
04/08/76	44985.8	Bill of sale to 2nd owner	Owner kept no records
07/08/82	103286.9	Bill of sale to 3rd owner	Owner kept no records
03/18/89	156236.8	Bill of sale to 4th owner	This owner restored car
04/22/91	58767.3	State inspection receipt	
05/15/91	58851.2	Bill of sale to 5th owner	

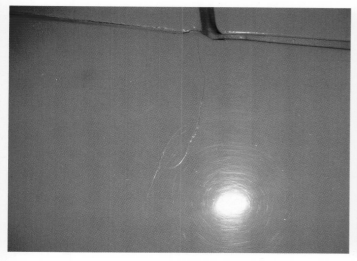

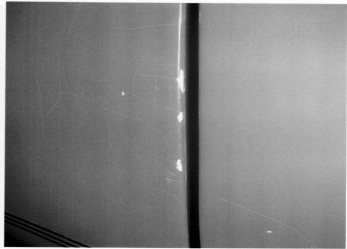

During your first trip around the car on the exterior inspection, examine the body panels for waves, ripples, rust, dents, and dings. Also, look for cracks in the paint. This crack radiates out from the upper corner of the trunk opening. This is a very common area to find problems, particularly on convertibles.

Work in a methodical manner, and check one panel at a time. Check the rear edge of the doors for chipping. These chips could be a sign the door is sagging. Cracks in the paint are a sign the substrate under the paint is unstable. This could be caused by poor preparation, rust, or age.

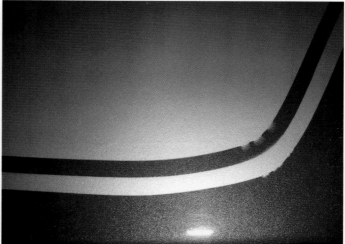

Look at the front fenders, as well as all panels, for obvious flaws like scratches, dents, or dings. Pay particular attention to the lower extremes, especially the corners. Tires throw dirt into these areas. This dirt then traps moisture, which forms rust. Leaking window seals will allow water to enter the doors and gather at the bottom, also causing rust.

Some collector cars were equipped with elaborate graphics. These graphics were either applied in a vinyl material or painted on. If they are painted on, look in the corners for flaws. When the graphics are taped out, the tape will have a tendency to lift in the corners, which allows paint to get underneath.

can only register up to 99,999 miles. Then they go back to 00,000. Most likely this car has 158,851.2 miles.

The fourth owner simply neglected to notify the state inspection facility that the vehicle actually had 100,000 miles more than indicated on the odometer. Was this an accidental omission? You would be surprised how much of this information is right under the buyer's nose, but they fail to see it. You may find other improprieties, such as an odometer reading that has not changed over several years or decades. This could

Very important areas to check are the rear quarter panels—particularly the lower portions. If this car leaked water around the rear window or the trunk lid, as many older cars did, this is likely to be where the damage would manifest itself. If it is a convertible, pay very, very close attention to this area.

Check the hood carefully because these large, horizontal panels can be subjected to all kinds of damage. People often place packages on their hoods. Check the front of the hood carefully for chips from road debris.

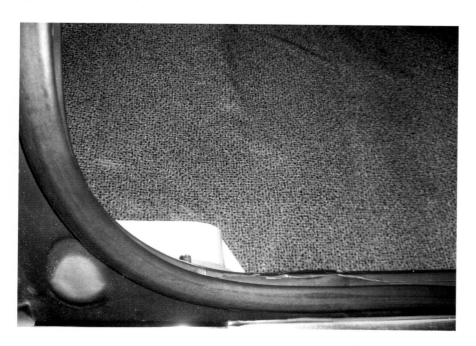

The trunk lid is another area people often place packages. Check the trunk lid for any distortion or obvious defects. The seal around the trunk lid should be checked carefully. It should be soft and flexible, with no tears. If the trunk lid does not seal properly, water will get into the trunk and cause rust.

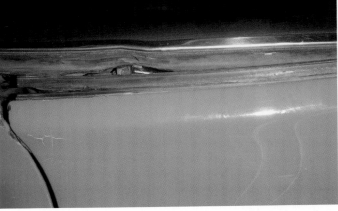

During the second trip around the car, on your exterior inspection, inspect all the chrome and stainless-steel trim for dents, dings, rust, scratches, pitting, peeling, and other obvious defects. Pieces like this drip rail molding are difficult to remove and overlooked during restoration.

Rubber molding and window seals are sometimes overlooked during restoration. They can be difficult to obtain and install. If they are not replaced, they will detract from the restoration. They will also allow water to enter and cause rust.

Grilles and hood trim take a lot of abuse from ordinary road hazards. Check them for chips and deterioration. Note the pitting on the chrome trim around the taillight of this 1962 Dodge Dart.

Moldings that protect the car's wheel openings are often dented and dinged. Unless the car is a popular make and model, these moldings can be very difficult to obtain.

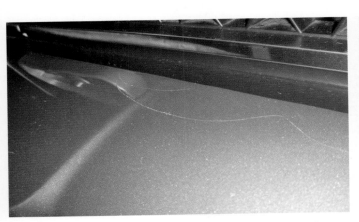

Needless to say, the front and rear bumpers must be inspected very carefully. They are called "bumpers" for a reason—the first line of defense against all sorts of dangers. If the car has chrome bumpers, look for pitting and rust. If the car has urethane bumpers, look for minor cracks in the paint. It only takes a small bump to crack the paint on the surface of these bumpers.

During the third trip around the car, inspect all glass, plastic, lenses, and emblems for scratches, cracks, fading, and other defects. Some of these defects may be difficult to spot. Notice the crack in the bottom taillight lens. This will be very difficult to see except under close inspection.

indicate a broken or disconnected odometer. It may also indicate the vehicle was stored for an extended period of time. After doing this exercise, you will have a much better sense of the car's history.

PERSONAL INSPECTION

Assuming you have satisfactorily completed your Checklist of Questions to Ask the Seller and your Checklist of Possible Documents, it is time to personally inspect the car. Completing this list will help you determine if you are interested in this particular car. It will also help you compare it with any other similar cars in which you might be interested. If possible, bring somebody with you. It's always nice to

Windshields often show scratches from old or missing wiper blades. These will generally appear as an arc across one or both sides of the windshield. Many replacement windshields for collector cars have been discontinued by the manufacturers for decades and are virtually impossible to find.

First Trip Checklist

On the first trip around the car during the exterior inspection, inspect the body panels for waves, ripples, and any other obvious defects like rust, dents, and dings.

- Driver's side door(s)
- Driver's side front fender
- View down the full length of the driver's side
- Header panel
- Hood
- View down the full length of the passenger side
- Passenger side front fender
- Passenger side door(s)
- Roof
- Passenger side rocker panel
- Passenger side rear quarter panel
- Trunk lid
- Driver's side rear quarter panel
- Driver's side rear door
- Driver's side rocker panel

Look closely at the emblems. Condition can vary greatly. Older emblems are often worn and faded. Sometimes they are missing completely. Small holes placed closely together are an indication an emblem should be there.

have a friend nearby, and it will be extremely helpful when checking items that require two people, such as reverse lights and turn signals.

This inspection should not intimidate you. Just complete it to the best of your ability. There are some terms with which you may be unfamiliar. Do the best you can, even if you don't know what an engine is. You may find the floral pattern used on the upholstery clashes with your favorite sundress. This may be enough for you to pass on this car.

Remember, if it turns out this is the car you are interested in, you will have it checked out by a mechanic or inspector anyway. However, there is no point paying a mechanic or inspector to look at this car until you've given it the once-over. Plan on taking approximately one hour to complete this inspection.

Ideally, all the headlights should match, although this is not critical. They should not have any stone chips. Dark areas behind the glass usually indicate the headlight is burnt out. Notice the misalignment of the trim above the headlights.

If, after completion of the exterior inspection, you feel the car is up to snuff, continue on to the interior inspection, which includes the trunk. Make sure there is a spare tire in the trunk and all related hardware. It is critical to lift the mat in the trunk and look for signs of dampness, rust, or repairs.

Have the door panels or side panels been cut in order to install speakers? Many of these panels are virtually unobtainable. If they have been cut, and originality is your goal, these panels can be very expensive to repair or replace.

Inspect the headliner carefully. Look for tears along the seams. Be sure to check above the sun visors. This is a favorite place for rodents to stand as they chew through the headliner to reach the padding inside. I've seen many cars with seemingly perfect headliners, only to find fist-sized holes when I've flipped down the sun visors. Sometimes a headliner can be repaired, but most often it will need to be replaced.

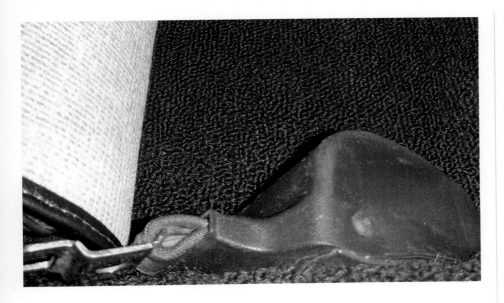

Moisture in a vehicle can cause any number of problems, from mold to rust. Check the carpeting carefully for dampness. The location of the dampness can indicate a leak in a rear window, convertible top, floor pan, or heater core. Any type of dampness warrants further investigation to determine the source of the leak and extent of the damage.

The exterior inspection comes first, and you'll begin by making three trips around the car in a clockwise direction, starting at the driver's side door. On the first trip, look at all of the body panels. On the second trip, look at all of the chrome and stainless-steel trim pieces. On the third trip, look at all of the glass, plastic, lenses, and emblems. Make sure all of the windows are up and the convertible top is up. Make notes of every little scratch or imperfection. These minor imperfections may not disqualify the car for potential purchase, but it will help you remember exactly what you have seen.

If at any time during the inspection, you are not happy with what you see, leave. Simply tell the seller, "It's not really what I'm looking for, but thanks for your time." If you are not happy with this car, it is not for you. If you, as a novice, are not happy with the condition, then a professional mechanic or inspector is not likely to be happy either.

Check all of the courtesy lights. These are usually activated by the headlight switch or when a door is opened. They are commonly found underneath the dash to illuminate the floors and in the door panels. They may also be found in the glove compartment and ashtray.

Second Trip Checklist

During the second trip around the car, on your exterior inspection, inspect all of the chrome and stainless steel trim. All collector cars have different types of trim, in varying locations, of different materials. It is impossible to list every single trim piece used on every collector car. You'll have to adapt this list to the car you are inspecting.

- Roof drip molding, driver's side
- Window edge trim, driver's side
- Side-view mirror housing, driver's side
- Body side molding, driver's side
- Rocker panel molding, driver's side
- Windshield trim
- Hood trim
- Front wheel opening molding, driver's side
- Fender top molding, driver's side
- Front bumper
- Fender top molding, passenger's side
- Front wheel opening molding, passenger's side

- Roof drip molding, passenger's side
- Window edge trim, passenger's side
- Side view mirror housing, passenger's side
- Body side molding, passenger side
- Rocker panel molding, passenger's side
- Rear window trim
- Quarter panel molding, passenger's side
- Rear wheel opening molding, passenger's side
- Rear bumper
- Quarter panel molding, driver's side
- Rear wheel opening molding, driver's side

Seat belts must operate properly and be free of tears and frays. In many states, collector cars are exempt from having to pass any emissions-related testing because of their age. However, most states do not exempt any cars from safety related testing. Seat belts are safety items and can cause a car to fail this test. Seat belts can be easily installed in any car that did not come with them.

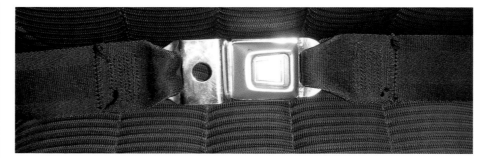

Operate all of the windows (including vent windows), whether manual or electric, to make sure they operate properly. Be sure to check that they go all the way up and down. Just one broken tooth in a window regulator can prevent it from operating properly.

Third Trip Checklist

During the third trip around the car, inspect all of the glass, plastic, lenses, and emblems for scratches, cracks, fading, and any other obvious defects.

- Front door glass, driver's side
- Side-view mirror glass, driver's side
- Windshield
- Front fender lenses/emblems, driver's side
- Grille
- Grille lenses/emblems
- Headlights
- Front fender lenses/emblems, passenger's side
- Side-view mirror glass, passenger's side
- Front and rear door glass, passenger's side
- Quarter panel lenses/emblems, passenger's side
- Rear window
- All rear bumper lenses
- Quarter panel lenses/emblems, driver's side
- Rear door glass driver's side

After completion of the exterior inspection, if you feel the car is up to snuff, continue on to the interior inspection, which includes the interior of the trunk as well as the interior of the vehicle itself. The interior inspection is not as structured as the exterior inspection, however, you should still do it in a thorough, orderly fashion to cover all items. Start with the inside rear of the car. Get in and make yourself comfortable.

The front seats will usually show the most signs of wear—especially the driver's seat. In addition to rips and tears, check for sagging in the seat bottoms. If the seats are electrically operated, check that they function properly throughout the range of their operation.

Interior Checklist

- Check the rear seat backs and bottoms for tears or sagging.
- Check the side panels or door panels. Have they been cut for speakers?
- Check the rear of the front seats for tears, cracks, or scuffs.
- Pick up floor mats, and check the carpeting underneath. Feel the carpeting with the palm of your hand. Is it damp? If the inside of the car has a musty smell, check the carpeting very carefully. This could indicate a leak in the rear window or the convertible top, or even a hole in the floor underneath the carpeting. The same applies to the trunk.
- Check the headliner. You should be able to see the complete headliner from the rear seat of the car.
- Check any courtesy lights that should work when the doors are open or when a switch is on.
- Check any rear speakers for proper operation. Call on your friend to operate the radio.
- Operate the rear windows, whether manual or electric, to make sure they operate properly.
- Check the seat belts, if so equipped, for tears and frays.
- Climb out of the back seat and get comfortable in the driver's seat.
- Check the front seat backs and bottoms for tears or sagging.
- Check the door panels. Have they been cut for speakers? Do the courtesy lights work?
- Pick up floor mats, and check the carpeting underneath. Particularly the driver's side. This is where most wear takes place. Once again, check for dampness.
- Check the kick panels. These are the panels on the side of the car, below the dash, in front of the doors. This is another common panel cut for speakers.
- Check the dashboard itself. Is the top dash pad cracked? Is the paint scratched? Are the lenses scratched or foggy?
- Start the engine. Do all of the gauges work? Listen for any unusual sounds, and observe if any smoke comes out of the exhaust pipe.
- Do all of the controls work? This includes slide controls for the heater/defroster/air conditioner and fan-speed switch.
- Do all switches work? This would include power windows, power door locks, power seats, power top, radio/stereo, trunk release, dome/courtesy lights.
- Does the parking brake work?
- Check all of the lights. Ask your friend to stand in front of the car and check the headlights, high beams, parking lights, and directional signals. Check the dashboard lights. This is also a good time to check the horn. Have your friend go to the back of the car and check all of the lights again. Don't forget the brake lights and reverse lights.
- Check the sun visors. They are often faded or cracked from the sun. Sometimes they are frozen in position and won't move at all.
- Open the ashtray and the glove compartment. Look inside. You never know what you'll find.
- Check the trunk. Once again check for dampness. If there is a musty smell, check very carefully. Look underneath the carpeting or trunk mat. Look (or feel) way down in the wells on both sides of the trunk. These areas are notorious for being damp.

If, after completion of the interior inspection, you feel this car is still a candidate, it is time for your mechanical inspection. Even though you may not be a mechanic, there are some things you can accomplish. Don't be concerned with any limitations you may have because a professional inspector or mechanic will complete the inspection in a thorough manner.

It's important to know your limitations. For example, it is common knowledge among car collectors that many Ford products of a certain era exhibit severe deterioration in the torque boxes and shock towers. Unfortunately, possession of this knowledge is of no use to 99 percent of these collectors because they don't know what a torque box or shock tower is.

Look carefully to see if the dash pad is cracked or if there are any signs of previous repairs. Minor cracks can generally be repaired. A severely cracked dash pad will need to be replaced at great expense. If an NOS or reproduction dash pad is not available, this one will have to be recovered at even greater expense.

Check the kick panels. These are the panels on the side of the car, below the dash, in front of the doors. They are called "kick panels" for a reason. This is an area that normally shows signs of wear and may have been cut for speakers.

Inspect the dashboard. Are the lenses clouded? Look at the chrome trim around the gauges. Often the dash is made of plastic, and the chrome flakes off after many years.

All switches should operate properly. This would include power top, windshield wipers, power windows, power door locks, power seats, trunk release, dome/courtesy lights, and horn.

All of the controls should be checked for proper operation. This includes slide controls for the heater/defroster/air conditioner and fan speed switch. Be sure to check if the radio operates properly. These controls can be expensive to repair because they typically operate on a combination of mechanical, electrical, and vacuum mechanisms.

Mechanical Checklist

Look at the tires. How is the tread? Look for cracks in the sidewalls. These cracks are very common on collector cars because collector cars are often driven very few miles. Tires, however, deteriorate from age and UV exposure. It is very common to find collector cars with tires that have 100 percent of their tread life still remaining, yet have deteriorated to the point they are unsafe to drive on. Look at the tread on the front tires. Are they worn evenly across the tread pattern? Uneven wear can indicate a problem with front suspension. Check the rear tires. There is nothing to stop a dishonest seller from switching the front and rear tires to try to hide this.

Open the hood and look for any obvious defects. Are there rust holes in the fender wells? Don't worry if you don't know what a fender well is. Are there rust holes in anything?

Is the engine dry, or is there oil all over the engine compartment? Or gasoline, or anti-freeze, or transmission fluid, or power steering fluid, or brake fluid? Once again, it doesn't matter if you know what these fluids look like. Is there any kind of fluid all over the engine compartment?

Look at any visible wires. Sections of wires wrapped in black plastic electrical tape are an indication of electrical repairs. Are there any bare wires? Are there any wires with loose ends that don't seem to go anywhere?

Are there any hoses leaking?

Are there any frayed belts?

Start the car and take it for a test ride. Did it start properly? How does it drive? Does the exhaust sound excessively loud? Does it shift smoothly? Does it pull to one side or the other? Does it pull to one side or the other when you apply the brakes? Does it have brakes? Are pieces falling off of it as you drive?

How do you feel driving it? Is your overall impression favorable?

The parking brake should operate smoothly and properly. This is one of those often overlooked items. It must be in proper working order to pass the safety inspection required in most states.

Above: Tires can give important clues to potential problems with a collector car. Uneven wear on the front tires can indicate worn suspension components. The tires should show even wear across the tread pattern. Check the rear tires. There is nothing to stop a dishonest seller from switching the front and rear tires to hide this.

Left: Open the hood and look for any obvious defects. Look at the belts, hoses, and wires. Does anything look worn or out of place? Are there any visible leaks? Is the battery secure? Is there any corrosion on the battery terminals?

TERMS

ANTIQUE CAR: Typically accepted as any vehicle 25 years old or older.

BASE COAT/CLEAR COAT: A method of refinishing a car in which a layer of clear paint is painted over color.

BUILD DATE: The specific date on which a vehicle or a component was manufactured

BUILD SHEET: A sheet that contains detailed information about which components were to be installed on a vehicle as it was being assembled. Often these were left in the vehicle after assembly was complete.

CAR SHOW: An organized event in which cars are typically sorted by class. Judging may or may not take place.

CAST CODE: A code that is cast into a component of a vehicle. These are typically found on major components of a vehicle and will sometimes contain manufacturer information.

CONSUMABLES: Parts of a vehicle that are intended to wear and must be replaced at periodic intervals.

CONVERTIBLE: A vehicle with a roof made of material that folds toward the rear of the car.

CROSSMEMBER: A structural component of a vehicle's frame or chassis meant to support the vehicle's body, suspension, or drivetrain.

CRUISE NIGHT: An informal get-together for the purpose of meeting with other car owners.

DAILY DRIVER: A vehicle that is intended to be used as a regular means of transportation with no limitations, as opposed to an antique, classic, or collectible car.

DATA PLATE: A tag affixed to a portion of the vehicle, typically the firewall, door jam, or inner fender, that contains data about that specific vehicle, usually in code form. Sometimes referred to as a trim tag.

DATE CODE: A code that gives information about the manufacture date of a vehicle component. It will typically be stamped into a component or stamped into a tag that will be affixed to a component.

DOCUMENTED: Intended to convey that some aspect of a vehicle's history is incontrovertible because it has been recorded either officially or unofficially.

FENDER TAG: A tag affixed to the inner fender or wheel housing that contains data about that specific vehicle, usually in code form. Sometimes referred to as a data plate.

FRAME: The structural portion of a vehicle to which other major components—body, suspension, or sub-frames—are attached.

FRAME-OFF RESTORATION: A restoration during which the body of the vehicle is removed from the frame.

FRAME-ON RESTORATION: A restoration during which the body of the vehicle is not removed from the frame.

HARDTOP: A vehicle on which the roof portion is supported only by the front windshield pillars and upper rear quarter panels.

MANUAL TRANSMISSION: A transmission in which the gears must be changed manually. Interchangeable with standard transmission.

MARQUE: A specific manufacturer of a vehicle. Sometimes used to denote a specific model.

OPTION: An item that was not standard equipment but was installed on a vehicle at the time that it was manufactured.

ORIGINAL BILL OF SALE: The bill of sale from the dealer to the original purchaser of the vehicle when it was new.

ORIGINAL WINDOW STICKER: The sticker that was affixed to the vehicle by the manufacturer when it was new. This would typically contain information like the V.I.N., optional equipment, and price.

PAPER TRAIL: The history, or portion of the history, of a vehicle that may be ascertained by using any or all of the information on its documents.

PATCH PANEL: A piece of sheet metal used to replace a damaged or rusted portion of a panel on a vehicle without replacing the complete panel.

PROVENANCE: Any known history about a vehicle. Typically, it needs to be verifiable to be valid.

RETRACTABLE: Similar to a convertible, except instead of a soft top that folds into the body of the car, the complete hard roof retracts and is stored within the body of the car, typically under the trunk lid.

SEDAN: A vehicle on which the roof portion is supported by the front windshield pillar, a post between the front and rear side windows (often referred to as a B pillar), and the upper rear quarter panels.

SERIAL NUMBER: A specific number assigned to an individual component of a car.

STANDARD TRANSMISSION: A transmission in which the gears must be changed manually. Interchangeable with manual transmission.

STRIPPED: The process by which material used to finish a car is removed. This can be accomplished by sanding, blasting, or through chemical means.

SUBFRAME: A structural component of a vehicle, other than the primary frame, to which major components of a vehicle may be affixed. Items that might attach to a subframe are an engine, transmission, or major suspension component.

TRIM TAG: A tag affixed to a portion of the vehicle—typically the firewall or door jamb—that contains data about that specific vehicle, usually in code form. Sometimes referred to as a data plate.

VIN: Vehicle Identification Number. A number assigned by a manufacturer unique to each individual vehicle.

VIN TAG: A tag that contains the VIN and is affixed to the vehicle by the manufacturer. Typical locations include the windshield pillar, dashboard, and door jam.

Index

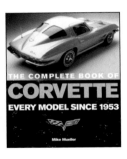

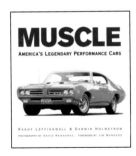

The Complete Book of Corvette:
Every Model Since 1953
ISBN 978-0-7603-2673-2

Motor City Dream Garages:
Amazing Collections from
America's Greatest Car City
ISBN 978-0-7603-2989-4

Muscle:
America's Legendary
Performance Cars
ISBN 978-0-7603-2284-0

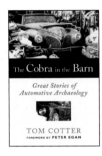
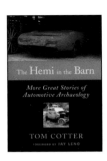

Ferrari:
Stories from Those
Who Lived the Legend
ISBN 978-0-7603-2833-0

The Cobra in the Barn:
Great Stories of
Automotive Archaeology
ISBN 978-0-7603-1992-5

The Hemi in the Barn:
More Great Stories of
Automotive Archaeology
ISBN 978-0-7603-2721-0

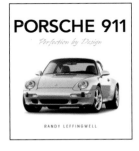

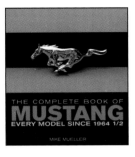

Porsche 911:
Perfection by Design
ISBN 978-0-7603-2975-7

McQueen's Machines:
The Cars and Bikes of
a Hollywood Icon
ISBN 978-0-7603-2866-8

The Complete Book of Mustang:
Every Model Since 1964 1/2
ISBN 978-0-7607-2838-5